PRAISE FOR
LOUISA ON THE FRONT LINES

"*Louisa on the Front Lines* is a lively account of a critical moment in Alcott's life, her time working as a nurse in the Civil War—a moment that reverberates, sometimes in surprising ways, in her most beloved work."
—Louisa Thomas, Author of *Louisa: The Extraordinary Life of Mrs. Adams*

"*Louisa on the Front Lines* tells the story of a powerful period in Louisa May Alcott's life—her brief occupation as a Civil War nurse. Samantha Seiple, with her lively, well-researched narrative, captures Alcott at a pivotal time in the history of our country and in her own career as a young writer. Readers will discover the story both engaging and informative. Alcott herself would have marveled at how Seiple's biographical and historical account reads like a novel!"
—Daniel Shealy, UNC Professor of English and Editor of the *Journals of Louisa May Alcott*

"*Louisa on the Front Lines* illuminates the working life of a wartime nurse—the stench, the rot, the supply shortages, the lack of respect shown nurses by male bureaucrats and doctors, the sheer horror of trying to care for young men whose bodies were mangled beyond repair. Strong and determined, Louisa May Alcott was tireless and loving as she tried to heal her patients or to be at their sides with comfort when they died. Not coincidentally, her experiences helped propel her to financial success as one of America's first professional women writers. Bravo to Samantha Seiple for her sensitive portrayal of the difficulties and the successes of Civil War nurses, as seen through the clear eyes of Louisa May Alcott."
—Dr. Patricia Brady, Historian and Biographer

LOUISA ON THE FRONT LINES

LOUISA MAY ALCOTT IN THE CIVIL WAR

SAMANTHA SEIPLE

SEAL PRESS

Cover design by Kerry Rubenstein
Cover image Bettmann Archive
Cover copyright © 2019 Hachette Book Group, Inc.

Seal Press
Hachette Book Group
1290 Avenue of the Americas, New York, NY 10104
www.sealpress.com
@sealpress

Printed in the United States of America

First Edition: February 2019

Published by Seal Press, an imprint of Perseus Books, LLC, a subsidiary of Hachette Book Group, Inc. The Seal Press name and logo is a trademark of the Hachette Book Group.

Library of Congress Cataloging-in-Publication Data
Names: Seiple, Samantha, author.
Title: Louisa on the front lines: Louisa May Alcott in the Civil War / Samantha Seiple.
Description: First edition. | New York, NY: Seal Press, 2019. | Includes bibliographical references and index.
Identifiers: LCCN 2018032967| ISBN 9781580058049 (hardcover) | ISBN 9781580058032 (ebook)
Subjects: LCSH: Alcott, Louisa May, 1832-1888. | Alcott, Louisa May, 1832-1888—Career in nursing. | Women authors, American—19th century—Biography. | United States—History—Civil War, 1861-1865—Hospitals. | United States—History—Civil War, 1861-1865—Women. | Military nursing—United States—History—19th century. Classification: LCC PS1018 .S45 2019 | DDC 813/.4 [B]—dc23
LC record available at https://lccn.loc.gov/2018032967

ISBNs: 978-1-58005-804-9 (hardcover), 978-1-58005-803-2 (ebook)

LSC-C

10 9 8 7 6 5 4 3 2 1

For Todd with love

CONTENTS

Mr. March did not go to the war, but Jo did.

—Louisa May Alcott [Jo March], responding to fans wanting
to know what is true in her beloved semiautobiographical
book, *Little Women*

THE HEROINE'S JOURNEY

URING THE HEIGHT OF THE HOLIDAY SEASON, IN December 1860, Louisa May Alcott and her neighbors in the tranquil town of Concord, Massachusetts, were buzzing with worry over the bitter divide of the United States. In November, Abraham Lincoln had won a contentious presidential election and had plans to prevent slavery in the westward-expanding nation. Shortly after he was elected, South Carolina was the first slave state to rebel and secede from the Union, and more Southern states were threatening to follow.

The Alcott family supported Lincoln, and if women had been allowed to vote, Louisa would have joined her father, Bronson, at the Concord Town Hall to cast her ballot. It was no secret that the Alcotts were red-hot abolitionists as well as feminists. They were outspoken and unwavering in their belief that men and women, regardless of race, deserved equal rights and opportunities.

Louisa was so passionate in her belief that when the Civil War broke out in April 1861, she wanted to be a soldier in the Union army. Since women weren't allowed to join the military, Louisa resigned herself to any opportunity to help abolish slavery and focused on more ladylike, acceptable pursuits, such as sewing uniforms for soldiers.

But then the door of opportunity opened just a crack, and Louisa was eager to push her way through. The Union army announced it was allowing women to be paid nurses, an unheard-of development at a time when it was not considered respectable work for a woman. Even so, practicality and the needs of wartime won out in this particular gender fight. The fierce and bloody battles of the war had resulted in an overwhelming number of casualties. There were too many sick and wounded and not enough male nurses to help, convincing the military to relent. Despite this new opportunity, there wasn't a mad rush of women signing up. Louisa, however, made the exceptional decision to enlist right away.

But Louisa wasn't from a typical family, and she wasn't a conventional woman. An avid runner—also unheard of for women at the time—and single still at age twenty-eight, her belief system had been shaped intellectually and emotionally by the environment she grew up in, and it was one of exceptional educational riches and desperate poverty. Her parents, who were friends with some of the greatest philosophers and reformers of the time, including Ralph Waldo Emerson, embraced ideals and beliefs that remain progressive by today's standards. Louisa had a front row seat watching her father and mother risk their livelihood, freedom, and lives hiding, teaching, and even living among freed and fugitive slaves.

But her father's self-absorption in pursuing his philosophical dreams and his careless disregard for his family's most basic needs of food, clothing, and shelter kept the Alcotts teetering on the brink of ruin. Louisa's mother tried to find work to support the family, but there were few respectable and profitable job opportunities for women. Many times, Louisa's mother felt like a beggar, having to ask her relatives again and again for money, writing, "My life is one of daily protest against the oppression and abuses of society."

While her mother fought for the family's survival, Louisa was writing her observations, thoughts, and feelings in her journals and letters. She was working on her plan to not only rescue her family from poverty but also to help drive change in the fight for human rights. Like her parents showed her, Louisa was going to lead by example.

The Civil War offered Louisa the opportunity to go to the front lines, where she would push the boundaries for women and test her beliefs, while gaining life experiences that would translate into an influential and lasting literary contribution—*Little Women*.

When it was first published in 1868, *Little Women* was a "radical manifesto." Louisa expertly wove her progressive beliefs and empathetic insights into her novel, creating original and unforgettable characters. *Little Women* was an instant best seller and has never been out of print. Millions of copies later (and counting), the trials and tribulations of the March sisters are still relatable, speaking universally to the hearts and minds of readers worldwide. Reading Louisa May Alcott's classic coming-of-age story is a rite of passage for most young girls, many of whom find themselves reading it again and again throughout their lifetime and passionately recommending it to the next generation of little women.

Part One

THE WAR AT HOME

Chapter 1

WAYWARD DAUGHTER

December 1860–February 1861, Concord, Massachusetts
A few months before the start of the Civil War

CHRISTMAS WASN'T CHRISTMAS WITHOUT PRESENTS. OR merrymaking. But twenty-eight-year-old Louisa May Alcott was, unfortunately, all too familiar with the grim reality of being "poor as rats" and nearly forgotten by everyone.

"We are used to hard times, and, as Mother says, 'while there is a famine in Kansas we mustn't ask for sugar-plums,'" Louisa, who was affectionately called Lu (or Louy) by her family and friends, noted in her journal.

Despite the crackling fire in the parlor, Christmas had been quiet and cheerless in the drafty clapboard house, which Lu jokingly called "Apple Slump"—much to the chagrin of her father. He preferred the name Orchard House, in honor of the apple trees he lovingly nurtured.

Even so, there had been fewer apples in the harvest this year, and, without the luxury of a furnace, it was impossible to stay warm inside Orchard House. The uncomfortable draft was just another reminder of Lu's situation.

But, several days later, when New Year's came around, Lu received a welcome surprise in the form of gifts from friends and acquaintances.

"A most uncommon fit of generosity seemed to seize people on my behalf," she wrote. "And I was blessed with all manner of nice things, from a gold and ivory pen to mince-pie and a bonnet."

When the holidays ended, though, the bleakness of winter settled in even further, and for the next several weeks Lu and the residents in her sleepy village of Concord, Massachusetts, experienced relentlessly frigid temperatures with a deep blanket of snow covering the ground. Those who dared to brave the cold were rewarded with the jingling of sleigh bells as horses trudged through the snow and seeing the children ice skating on Goose Pond.

The first slight thaw of the winter occurred on February 2, 1861, and, on that morning, Lu woke up at dawn and took her daily run. Even though most women were forbidden to run—it was considered unladylike and downright dangerous—Lu threw caution to the bitter wind. She loved running, and her parents encouraged physical exercise. For Lu, not only did running make her feel free but it was a spiritual experience, making her feel closer to God.

So Lu wasn't worried about what her neighbors would think. By now, they were used to seeing her run with the deftness of a deer through the open meadow near Orchard House and into Walden Woods, with only the sound of her feet pattering and her petticoat ruffling. When Lu was a child, no boy could be her friend until she outran him in a race. Lu's physical strength and endurance made her seem different from other women, but she was considered the most beautiful and fastest runner in Concord.

After her run, Lu sat down at her desk, which was shaped like a half moon and positioned between two windows. Her father, who was an accomplished carpenter, had made the writing desk especially for her.

Lu was working feverishly on a novel, a love-triangle romance she called *Moods*. She was using her new gold and ivory pen, dipping it carefully into her inkstand and trying not to get too much ink on her fingers. She didn't want to accidentally stain her red merino dress.

New clothes were hard to come by, and most of her dresses were hand-me-downs from her wealthy cousins and friends. Lu had worn her last silk dress for six years, mending it so many times it was "more patch and tear than gown."

When Lu finally had a little extra money, she bought some wine-colored wool and sewed the red gown herself. The dress was nice but not nice enough for all occasions. Just before Christmas, Lu turned down an invitation to the one-year anniversary meeting of John Brown's death because she didn't have a "good gown" to wear.

The radical abolitionist Brown had been a close family friend of the Alcotts, who were themselves active and outspoken abolitionists. Lu and her family believed in complete racial equality, including interracial marriage. They attended antislavery meetings and put their own freedom on the line as participants in the secret and illegal Underground Railroad. For as long as Lu could remember, her family had harbored fugitive slaves.

When Lu was fourteen years old, a runaway slave stayed with them for a week and ate his meals at their table before leaving for Canada. Her father recorded in his journal, "We supplied him with the means of journeying, and bade him a good godspeed to a freer land.... His stay with us has given image and a name to the dire entity of slavery, and was an impressive lesson to my children, bringing before them the wrongs of the black man and his tale of woes." Throughout her life, Lu had met many of the legendary leaders who were risking their lives to abolish slavery—from Harriet Tubman, who stayed at the Alcott home, to Frederick Douglass.

So, when John Brown was executed for trying to arm a slave rebellion, the Alcotts considered him a martyr and saint. "Glad I have lived to see the Antislavery movement and this last heroic act in it," Lu wrote after Brown led the Harpers Ferry raid. "Wish I could do my part in it."

To honor the one-year anniversary of John Brown's death, Lu decided to write a poem in the midst of working on *Moods*. But she couldn't find the right words to express her feelings, and she didn't think it was any good, lamenting, "I'm a better patriot than poet." Even so, she sent it out anyway, and, according to her notes from the time, it was published in a newspaper.

Whenever Lu sat down at her desk to write, she liked to wear an old green and red party shawl, which she called her "glory cloak." It kept her warm and helped protect her dress from ink stains. It matched the brimless green silk hat that her mother, Abba (later known as Marmee), had made for her and adorned with a red bow.

Lu's hat covered her long, chestnut-colored hair, which, when it wasn't pinned up in a simple, becoming style, nearly touched the floor. It was her favorite, and, in her opinion, best feature. "If I look in my glass, I try to keep down vanity about my long hair, my well-shaped head, and my good nose," Lu revealed in her journal. She could remember a time when her family was so desperate for money that she had seriously considered cutting off her hair and selling it to a wigmaker. "I went to a barber, let down my hair, and asked him how much he would give me for it," she said to a friend. "When he told me the sum, it seemed so large to me that I then and there determined I would part with my most precious possession if during the next week the clouds did not lift."

But on that particular occasion, a family friend came to the rescue. "That was not the first time he had helped father, nor was it indeed the last," Lu said. That friend was Ralph Waldo Emerson. He and his family lived down the road from the Alcotts, not far from Henry David Thoreau, another one of their good friends. Like Emerson and Thoreau, Lu's father was a transcendentalist.

Although the most influential philosophers of the transcendentalist movement at the time lived in the small village of Concord, most of the townspeople didn't really understand what the term "transcendental" meant. But they did consider it completely unorthodox. It was a radical notion at that time to believe in a direct relationship with God and a oneness with nature, and that a divine spirit is present in every human and in all of nature. As a transcendentalist, Bronson stuck fiercely to his principles, not caring about money or material things, even if it meant that his family went hungry.

"Philosophers are always poor," Lu wrote. "And too modest to pass round their own hats."

Although Bronson was not as famous as Emerson and hadn't attended Harvard University like Emerson (and Thoreau), his loyal and well-respected friend looked up to him and considered him "the most transcendental of the Transcendentalists." Bronson's ideas had influenced Emerson in his defining essay, *Nature*, which launched Emerson's career. He had paraphrased passages from Bronson's journals, and considered him a genius and half god. Emerson believed that Bronson was the one philosopher who could have held a conversation with Plato. But he also likened Bronson to Don Quixote—a naïve and impractical idealist. Unlike Emerson, others looked down on Bronson, calling him a fool, a madman, pompous, and, perhaps even worse, a bore.

BRONSON'S CONNECTION to the transcendentalists ran so deep that Emerson even had a hand in the family's geography. In 1845, when the Alcotts were living forty-five miles west of Boston near the rural town of Harvard and Bronson found himself out of work, Emerson urged him to move to Concord, closer to Boston, and even helped him buy a home. When the Alcotts moved into their house on Lexington Road, the villagers were atwitter with worry, casting a suspicious eye and shunning the Alcotts. Bronson's reputation as "a fanatic in belief and habit" had preceded him.

Early in his career, he had made a name for himself as a schoolteacher—and not always in a good way. Bronson, who was the oldest son of an illiterate farmer, lacked a high school and college degree. But when he wasn't working with his father on the family farm, his doting mother had taught him to read and write. The only formal education he received was when he earned a scholarship to Cheshire Academy, a private prep school that admitted boys *and* girls. Although he yearned to learn, when he found himself surrounded by better-dressed students from more privileged backgrounds, Bronson didn't feel worthy, more like a country bumpkin, and left after a short time. Despite dropping out of school, he would later earn his teaching certificate and spend his lifetime feeding his intellect—and prove to be a trailblazer with his ideas of education reform.

But, like many trailblazers, his progressive ideas would also be his undoing. Bronson's teaching methods were considered radical at a time when children learned by rote memorization and strict discipline. Bronson believed that education should inspire the mind and awaken the soul. He came up with the idea of recess, and, in the classroom, instead of encouraging memorization, he tried to engage his students in discussions and draw out their ideas.

Instead of using physical punishment, Bronson handled discipline problems by discussing them as a group with his pupils. Sometimes Bronson would extend his hand and tell the misbehaving student to strike it because it was he who had failed as a teacher. Bronson believed this instilled shame and triggered feelings of guilt, so the behavior would, in theory, stop.

Many people thought his teaching ideas were ridiculous. Regardless, the school he opened in Boston in 1834 was successful for six years. Defying the common belief that girls didn't need an education, half of his twenty students were girls (two of whom were his daughters Anna and Lu). But Bronson was ahead of his time, and when he allowed an African American child to enroll in the all-white school, the parents quickly withdrew their children. Soon after, Bronson's school closed, leaving his family thousands of dollars in debt.

Bronson took an active part in caring for his daughters, which was also unheard of at the time. He carefully observed their behavior and kept detailed records of their development, believing that children were born into the world morally perfect, "trailing clouds of glory." His wife, Abba, agreed.

Unfortunately for Lu, her parents' high ideals meant that they expected perfection from her. Any flaw must be fixed. They didn't see people for who they were but for how far they fell short of who they should be. Lu did not fit neatly into her father's ideas. Rebellious, willful, and short tempered, Lu was all action, tearing through the house, making noise, pulling her older sister Anna's hair, climbing and falling out of trees, and running away from home.

When Lu was three and a half years old, he recorded her behavior in his journal: "Father, mother, sister, objects all are equally defied, and not infrequently the menace terminates in blows.... Sitting with me today Louisa held my hand in hers, and while enjoying the sense of bodily contact, she seemed to be instinctively tempted to pinch me."

To tame Lu's "wild exuberance of a powerful nature," Bronson used "discipline mingling severity and kindness." This meant Lu received spankings—even though her father said he didn't believe in corporal punishment. But, instead of making him question his pious self-image as a child-rearing expert and his unrealistic expectations of his daughter, he blamed his wife. "I do not believe in its [spanking] efficacy except as a corrective discipline," he explained in his journal. "Had the children been under my supervision continually...I do not believe it would have been necessary to resort to such methods."

Bronson rarely had to punish Anna, whom he favored. He thought fair-haired, blue-eyed Anna resembled and acted more like him, while dark-haired Lu looked and acted more like her mother. Anna was a "good girl"; she was delicate and listened to her father, trying to please him and complying with his rules. Bronson noted in his journal, "She listened to what I was saying, and after I had finished, putting her arms around me, she said, 'I like you!'"

Unlike Lu, who defiantly broke the rules and expressed her frustration with a fiery temper, just like her mother. Bronson complained further about Lu in his journal, "She only looks toward the objects of her desires and steers proudly, adventurously . . . toward the heaven of her hopes. The stronger the opposing gale, the more sullenly and obstinately does she ply her energies."

Viewing his children as an extension of himself and focusing on his need to mold them into his idea of perfection, Bronson was unable to see that Lu's fierce determination in the face of opposition wasn't a flaw. It was in fact the perfect trait to nurture the seed of her ambition and help it bloom. Bronson's disapproval and rejection of Lu caused her to look back on her childhood and think that she was "the worst child ever known," especially when he called her a "demon."

Always known for her quick wit and humor, Lu tried to make light of the criticism by signing her letters to her father "Ever your loving demon." But the constant criticism and rejection emotionally wounded her, making her believe she wasn't good enough. Lu wanted her father's approval and love, as well as her mother's. It wouldn't be until after her father's next failed experiment that Lu would figure out how she was going to get it.

In 1843, her father had decided to cofound a utopian society, a new Eden, based on transcendental beliefs when Lu was ten years old, following the failure of his school in Boston. He moved the family to a run-down farmhouse in Harvard and named the communal farm Fruitlands even though, as Lu wryly noted, there was no orchard. But the name Fruitlands reflected the strict rule that no one on the premises was allowed to eat meat or dairy products of any kind. "No animal substances neither flesh, butter, cheese, eggs, nor milk pollute our tables, nor corrupt our bodies," wrote a member of Fruitlands. The only acceptable fruits and vegetables where those that grew above ground, toward heaven, such as apples. Root vegetables, such as potatoes, which grew underground and, in Bronson's mind, toward hell, were forbidden.

The members weren't allowed to use animals for farm labor or manure for fertilizer. Although Bronson grew up on a farm, he couldn't see that his strict ideals were impractical and unrealistic. Without oxen or horses to help plow the fields, there weren't enough laborers to grow the food needed to become self-sufficient.

At one time, there was a total of fourteen members at Fruitlands, but Bronson and the other philosophers were often gone, traveling around trying to recruit more members. He left his wife behind with the burden of caring for their four young daughters along with the labor-intensive farming and housework. Isolated and overworked with no source of income, Abba was miserable and afraid she was losing her mind, writing in her journal, "Circumstances most cruelly drive me from the enjoyment of my domestic life.... I am almost suffocated in this atmosphere of restriction.... I hope the experiment will not bereave me of my mind.... [T]his [is an] invasion of my rights as a woman and a mother."

Young Lu also hated Fruitlands and poured her heart out in her journal. "More people coming to live with us; I wish we could be together, and no one else. I don't see who is to clothe and feed us all, when we are so poor now. I was very dismal, and then went to walk and made a poem."

Bronson's experiment lasted for six months before it failed. Besides the Alcott family, the number of members had dwindled to two. "He was very strict, indeed rather despotic, in his rule of community.... They were nearly starved to death ... [and] would have perished with hunger if they had not furtively gone among the surrounding farmers and begged for food," ex-members told a reporter.

The unforgiving New England winter was upon them, and they were running out of firewood. They were not allowed to use fabric made from animals or harvested with slave labor, but their linen clothes were not warm enough for them to survive the winter. Still, Bronson stubbornly clung to his ideals and considered joining the nearby Shaker settlement, a religious community with a communal farming system and profitable woodworking business. The only caveat was the Shakers separated family members by gender and age, so the Alcotts would be required to live separate lives, seeing their children only once a year.

"I was very unhappy, and we all cried.... I prayed God to keep us all together," Lu wrote at the time in her journal. (Years later, she would comment, "Little Lu began to feel the family cares and peculiar trials.... She never forgot this experience, and her little cross began to grow heavier from this.")

But, in the end, Lu's mother refused to join the Shaker community. She planned on leaving her husband and taking her daughters with her. "The arrangements here [at Fruitlands] have never suited me, and I am impatient to leave all behind.... My duties have been arduous, but my satisfaction small," Abba wrote.

For Bronson, it was a difficult decision. He didn't want to compromise his principles, but he ultimately decided not to join the Shakers in order to keep his family together.

However, Bronson was so overwhelmed with disappointment and grief over his failed utopia that he went on a hunger strike and refused to get out of bed. For months, his wife had been questioning her husband's mental state and confided to her brother in a letter, "I do not allow myself to despair of his recovery, but oh, Sam that piercing thought flashes through my mind of insanity, and a grave, yawning to receive his precious body, would be to me a consolation compared to that condition of life."

All the same, Abba was left scrambling, trying to figure out how to make money. She didn't want to sell her silver teapot and spoons, but her extended family was tired of her asking for money to pay off their mounting debts. The seemingly never-ending cycle of indebtedness to family members began years ago when Bronson's own father, a hardworking farmer, sold off part of his farm to settle his son's first big debt. Abba's father, an enterprising merchant, stopped giving them money after it was evident Bronson didn't intend to pay him back.

When Abba's brother, Samuel, asked why Bronson thought a paying job was beneath him, Abba explained that Bronson didn't believe he should accept wages—only donations—which limited his job prospects. "No one will employ him in his way," she told her brother in a letter. "He cannot work in theirs, if he thereby involve his conscience. He is resolved in this matter that I believe he will starve or freeze before he will sacrifice principle to comfort." Despite her misgivings, the relentless strain on their marriage, and her impulse to leave him because of the Fruitlands debacle, Abba was loyal and supportive of her "visionary" husband. She not only considered him a genius and morally superior but also her savior.

WHEN SHE first met the tall, blond, blue-eyed teacher, with a polished gentlemanly manner and a penchant for beautiful clothes, she was twenty-six years old, a spinster at the time, living with her brother. Although she'd been engaged previously, her fiancé had died unexpectedly. Abba wanted to find love and have a family of her own, and she was immediately taken by the quiet and charismatic budding philosopher. But Abba May came from a prominent Boston family, a descendent of the distinguished Quincys and Sewalls, which included John Hancock, the signer of the Declaration of the Independence, in its extended family. This made Bronson painfully aware of his humble beginnings, growing up a poor country boy whose mother was known to enjoy an unwomanly corncob pipe. He had worked hard over the years educating himself and refining his rough edges.

Despite their stark contrasts, Abba pursued him, encouraged by her brother, who wrote, "Don't distress yourself about his poverty. His mind and heart are so much occupied with other things that poverty and riches do not seem to concern him." And, despite their contrasting personalities, they decided to get married. "He is moderate, I am impetuous—He is prudent and humble—I am forward and arbitrary. He is poor—but we are both industrious—why may we not be happy?" she confided in a letter to Samuel.

But Abba couldn't see that hidden underneath Bronson's seemingly serene and pious exterior lurked a destructive fatal flaw. Bronson exhibited traits of a covert narcissist, and his self-absorption always caused him to prioritize his needs before those of anyone else, including his family.

"Wife, children, and friends are less to him than the great ideas he is seeking to realize," Abba admitted in her journal, eleven years into her marriage and a few months before moving to Fruitlands.

Bronson clung to the grandiose idea that he was more enlightened and had a higher purpose than everyone else. His philosophy was going to change the world, and Bronson's narcissistic need to maintain the Christlike image he had of himself, instead of placing his family's most basic needs first, was going to keep his wife and daughters stranded in emotional and financial poverty. The family was often forced to rely on the generosity of others, friends and neighbors who left baskets of food on their doorstep, gave old dresses to the girls, and discreetly provided money. "It is this dependence on others which is the worm gnawing at the vitals of my tranquility," Abba wrote in a letter.

After the Fruitlands disaster, and Bronson's emotional and financial abandonment of his family, Abba and her daughters were left to fend for themselves. "I have no accomplishments," Abba noted to her brother. "For I never was educated for a fine lady, but I have handicraft, *wit*, and *will* enough to feed the body and save the souls of myself and children."

Abba worked tirelessly trying to put food on the table and keep a roof over their heads. But respectable job opportunities for women were scarce. For the next few years, she took in sewing and boarders, tried but failed to start a school, and even left her family behind to work as the matron of a water-cure spa in Maine.

Through friends, she finally found a respectable job in Boston helping the poor as the city's first paid social worker. Abba, like Bronson, was always trying to help others whom she considered worse off than herself, even if it meant their children went without a meal.

"She always did what came to her in the way of duty and charity, and let pride, taste, and comfort suffer for love's sake," Lu commented.

The Alcott home was "a shelter for lost girls, abused wives, friendless children, and weak or wicked men," Lu recorded in her journal. "Father and Mother had no money to give, but gave them sympathy, help, and if blessings would make them rich, they would be millionaires. This is practical Christianity."

Eventually, Abba opened an employment office, trying to help "good girls" find jobs as cooks, parlor maids, seamstresses, and dressmakers. For a subscription of one dollar, the client was entitled to choose from the pool of prospective employees for the duration of six months.

"It was not fit work for her," Lu noted. "But it paid."

Meanwhile, Lu's father was trying to articulate his philosophical ideas for publication, but he was a more gifted talker than writer. He would spend months on the road giving lectures. But these endeavors were not profitable, and one time he brought home only one dollar.

Abba's practicality and quest to earn money greatly influenced Lu, feeding her growing ambition. Abba's struggle was

Lu's living example that women deserved better-paying jobs and equal rights. Her mother was also very vocal about women's right to vote, writing a petition and sending it to the state legislature in 1852 (it was rejected). Lu's father was a role model too, influencing her belief that a woman should be self-reliant. Abba reinforced these beliefs by encouraging Lu and her sisters to learn a trade as they sought work to support the family. "My girls *shall* have trades," Abba informed her brother.

WHEN LU was twelve years old, she realized that her sewing skills could make her money. She started making clothes for dolls and selling them to the neighborhood children. The tiny, soft brimless hats she made were all the rage. "To the great dismay of the neighbors' hens," Lu recalled, "who were hotly hunted down, that I might tweak out their downiest feathers to adorn the dolls' headgear."

A year later, thirteen-year-old Lu figured out how she was going to win her parents' love and approval. "I have made a plan for my life, as I am in my teens, and no more a child," Lu wrote. "I am old for my age and don't care much for girl's things. People think I'm wild...but Mother understands and helps me. I have not told any one about my plan; but I'm going to *be* good." Her strategy to be good was to be rich and take care of her family—to rescue them from poverty. To "be a help and a comfort, not a care and a sorrow," especially to her hardworking and self-sacrificing mother whom she wanted to have "every wish granted."

But, as Lu grew older, she was still a wild and irrepressible tomboy, which was not how a young woman was supposed to behave. Her father, who didn't approve of her plan to be rich, continued to be sharply critical of his mercurial and mercenary daughter. Lu was resigned that she was the bad one.

Her older sister, Anna, was proper, virtuous, dutiful, and self-sacrificing. Lu's younger sister, Lizzie, was the saintlike "good" one (shy and serene like Bronson). Lu's youngest sister, May, who had pretty blond curls, was the "baby" of the family and a little vain and selfish, but things always seemed to go her way.

Lu expressed her pain in her journal, "My quick tongue is always getting me into trouble, and my moodiness makes it hard to be cheerful when I think how poor we are, how much worry it is to live, and how many things I long to do I never can. So every day is a battle, and I'm so tired I don't want to live; only it's cowardly to die till you have done something."

Despite the disapproval (or possibly because of it) Lu didn't give up on her plan. She started working outside their home when she was fifteen and wasn't afraid to try her hand at different jobs, even working as a servant when she was eighteen years old. She was hired out through her mother's employment agency. Her service job scandalized her wealthy relatives, much to Lu's delight, considering her rebellious streak. But her job as a hired companion was not what it seemed and turned out to be a humiliating experience, which would negatively affect her attitude toward men. Lu rarely talked about it, but, when she did, there would be tears in her eyes.

The lawyer who hired her, James Richardson, wanted more than a servant to look after his ailing sister and father. After finishing the housework, he wanted Lu to sit at his feet and listen to him while he spoke philosophically and made romantic overtures. When Lu refused him, he assigned her the roughest chores to do—chopping wood, carrying heavy buckets of water from the well, and shoveling snow.

It was the hardest work Lu ever did. But she was determined to stay, which she did for seven weeks. Lu had made a promise, and she didn't want to go back on her word. She also wanted to give her mother enough time to find a replacement.

The bad experience was made worse when Lu was paid a paltry four dollars. The experience made Lu feel like "a galley slave," and the insight reinforced her belief in equal rights—for slaves and women. And it didn't make her waver in her determination to find a job and be paid what she was worth.

"I will do something, by and by. Don't care what, teach, sew, act, write, anything to help the family; and I'll be rich and famous and happy before I die, see if I won't!"

Ever since Lu was a teenager, she'd been writing stories and poems and sending them to publishers, which was a respectable way for a woman to earn good money. Her family encouraged her to write. At sixteen, she wrote a book of fairy tales, which was published six years later. "My book came out," Lu recorded in her journal. "And people began to think that topsy-turvy Louisa would amount to something after all." Lu didn't get rich from her book; she made thirty-five dollars, but throughout the years she kept trying to get more work published. Eventually, the most prestigious literary magazine at the time, the *Atlantic Monthly*, bought a story she'd submitted, called "Love and Self-Love," and she was paid fifty dollars. Then they bought two more, "A Modern Cinderella" and "Debby's Debut," for seventy-five dollars and fifty dollars, respectively. "After ten years of hard climbing I had reached a good perch on the ladder," Lu wrote.

In retrospect, Lu knew that getting married could have easily helped her family with its financial struggles. But, at twenty-eight years old, Lu was well past the marrying age and considered herself a spinster. But she was a spinster by choice. She'd had suitors and a marriage proposal, which she turned down, preferring her independence. "I'd rather be a free spinster and paddle my own canoe," she wrote.

Her parents' marriage had soured her on the idea. When Lu was seventeen years old, she wrote about how she believed marriage had affected her mother: "I often think what a hard life she has had since she married—so full of wandering and all sorts of worry! So different from her early easy days, the youngest and most petted of her family. I think she is a very brave, good woman; and my dream is to have a lovely, quiet home for her, with no debts or troubles to burden her. But I'm afraid she will be in heaven before I can do it."

So, ON that cold February morning in 1861 with a slight thaw outside, Lu sat at her desk, wrapped in her glory cloak, and worked as quickly as she could, trying to finish her novel. It was her second try at it. The first novel she wrote, *The Inheritance*, was gathering dust. But Lu was holding onto the hope that her writing would make her rich. She was completely absorbed in her work, weaving her transcendental ideas into the story line, basing two of her characters on Emerson and Thoreau, both of whom Lu had secretly loved as a girl.

But she was not completely satisfied with it yet. Trying to maintain her focus on the task at hand, Lu rarely left her chair, and she barely slept or ate. Her mother would quietly bring her cups of tea, and her father would leave her red apples to eat and hard cider to drink, allowing Lu to work until her head was dizzy and her legs were shaky.

Although, as a rule, Lu didn't like interruptions when she was writing, she did make an exception when someone was sick. Only then would she drop everything. This happened when her mother fell ill the previous month, after the New Year. "I corked up my inkstand and turned nurse," Lu wrote. "The dear woman was very ill, but rose up like a phoenix from her ashes."

This wasn't Lu's first time nursing a sick family member. A few years before, her younger sister Lizzie was stricken with scarlet fever. She couldn't seem to recover and suffered from a bright red rash all over her body coupled with a fever, sore throat, vomiting, and hair loss. The Alcotts turned to doctors, but none of their diagnoses or medicines helped. "It seems to me that the system of medicine is a prolonged *Guess*," Lu's mother wrote.

One doctor finally told them there was no hope. "A hard thing to hear," Lu wrote in her journal. "But if she is only to suffer, I pray she may go soon." Lu stayed by Lizzie's bedside during the night, keeping watch and allowing their mother to rest. As the doctor predicted, Lizzie continued to get worse. On March 14, 1858, Lu wrote in her journal, "My dear Beth [Lizzie] died at three this morning.... For two days she suffered much, begging for ether, though its effect gone.... [S]he lay in Father's arms, and called us round her.... [S]he bid us good-by...held our hands and kissed us tenderly." Lu and her mother washed and dressed Lizzie's body for the burial. "She is well at last," Lu wrote in a letter to a friend.

It was now nearly three years after Lizzie's death, and Lu and her family were still trying to pay off the medical bills. But the experience of nursing sick family members had made an impression on Lu. After Lizzie's death, Lu mused in her journal: "Wonder if I ought not be a nurse, as I seem to have a gift for it. Lizzie, [cousin] L[ouisa] W[illis], and Mother all say so; and I like it. If I couldn't write or act I'd try it. May yet."

Chapter 2

STITCHES

April 19, 1861, Concord, Massachusetts
One week after the start of the Civil War

A BLANKET OF DARK CLOUDS HUNG IN THE SKY, BUT THE threat of a storm didn't stop Lu, or the entire village of Concord for that matter, from swarming outside Town Hall in Monument Square, across from Wright's Tavern, on the corner where Main Street and Lexington Road meet.

Seven days prior, on April 12, the first shots of the Civil War had been fired at Fort Sumter in Charleston, South Carolina. "The Confederate Traitors have commenced the war…and their first prize in [the] fight…has been the capture of Fort Sumter and sixty men.…This inglorious success will cost them," the *Evening Star* in Washington, DC, declared.

When the details of the fight were first telegraphed to Washington, President Abraham Lincoln ordered the Second Cavalry to protect the capital against a surprise attack, stopping just short of martial law. The threat that the city might fall into the hands of the Confederacy prompted Lincoln to issue a proclamation calling for a force of 75,000 volunteers. "The call for troops will be zealously responded to.... The war, which the rebels have insanely begun, is a terrible necessity. Let it be as short as possible," the newspaper reported.

Soon after Lincoln called for volunteers, the town of Concord organized the Concord Artillery of the Fifth Regiment, Massachusetts Volunteer Militia, and started to collect money to support the soldiers in the field and their families left behind at home. Within twenty-four hours, they raised $5,000, exceeding their expectations. Some couldn't believe it. Emerson's daughter Ellen wrote that she'd heard "Concord had raised $4,000 for the families of the company. I suppose that is an exaggeration, for $2,000 was thought a wonderful sum." But the start of the war had "kindled a patriotic rage that envelopes all parties and all classes throughout the Union States."

Lu was no different. While she watched the Concord Artillery, she wished she could join them. "I long to be a man, but as I can't fight, I will content myself with working for those who can," Lu wrote. She worked alongside the other women in Concord knitting socks and sewing uniforms. "A busy time getting them ready, and a sad day seeing them off, for in a little town like this we all seem like one family in times like these."

While the American flag was raised and securely attached to a flagstaff made from a tree from the forest made famous by Thoreau's *Walden*, the crowd sang "The Star Spangled Banner." There was a feeling like bottled lightning electrifying the crowd. A prayer was said, the cannon was fired, and bells rang out. People were cheering and crying.

It was half past one o'clock when the train whistled, signaling everyone that it was time to say good-bye to the forty-five men and boys who made up the Concord Artillery. The newly enlisted soldiers fell in line, ready to march to Concord's rather plain-looking train depot, near Henry David Thoreau's home in town.

Standing in the crowd, Lu watched as their captain, George Prescott, who was born and raised in Concord, lifted his sword. But before he could shout his marching order, his wife broke free from the crowd and rushed toward him, kissing him good-bye. When the Concord Artillery started marching, kicking up dust on Main Street, everyone followed. "At the station the scene was very dramatic, as the brave boys went away perhaps never to come back again," Lu wrote.

Stuck at home, Lu tried to return to her writing but was soon distracted. "John Brown's daughters came to board, and upset my plans of rest and writing.... I had my fit of woe... then put my papers away, and fell to work at housekeeping. I think disappointment must be good for me, I get so much of it," Lu noted. Eighteen-year-old Annie and fifteen-year-old Sarah Brown were in Concord to attend a school run by a fervent abolitionist named Frank Sanborn, who had been arrested after John Brown's raid at Harpers Ferry. He was accused of being one of the "Secret Six" who helped finance Brown's raid. But Sanborn's neighbors and friends, many part of the Underground Railroad, rallied around him, and with the help of Senator Rockwood Hoar, he was released from custody.

The Alcotts were among Sanborn's supporters, considering his actions heroic. And Sanborn had a great respect for Bronson and his principles. He used his influence as the head of the Concord school board to offer Bronson the job of school superintendent. Bronson accepted the job but only after the school board agreed to afford him the freedom to instill his progressive ideas. He visited the schools and wrote reports for the school board, expressing his forward-thinking ideas, such as the belief that girls should have an equal chance at education like boys. But the pay was meager at one hundred dollars a year, not enough to support his family. So, the Alcotts occasionally took in boarders to earn additional money.

Since Lu's youngest sister, May, was teaching in Syracuse, New York, and her older sister, Anna, was married and living in Cambridge, Lu helped her mother with the domestic chores. But she hated doing housework. "They are good for me I've no doubt but... [i]f I lived alone I should make the beds once a week, clean house every ten years, & never cook at all which would simplify things grandly," Lu revealed. Lu and her mother did have help with the laundry, but they did the ironing themselves, which usually meant folding the clothes with a "brush and a promise"—unless it was one of Bronson's shirts. Lu's mother always made sure that her husband's shirts were neatly pressed, just how he liked them. This left a lasting impression on Annie Brown. "I used to think that if Mr. Alcott's philosophy had made him wear a few less clean shirts, that his wife might have rested instead of toiling and sweating over the ironing board so long to pamper his fastidious notions," she wrote.

In the evenings, after dinner was served and the dishes were washed, Lu and her mother would have lively discussions with Annie and Sarah while playing games. Some of their favorites were cribbage, chess, casino, and old maid. One time during the discussions, Annie asked Lu why she hadn't married a man who was obviously interested in her. "Ah, he is too blue [puritanical] and too prudent for me, I should shock him constantly," Lu replied.

On Monday evenings, the Alcott home was open to their friends, and many times students from Sanborn's school, like

Emerson's son, Edward, and Nathaniel Hawthorne's son, Julian, stopped by. They would join in on the parlor games and discussions, and just after ten o'clock, Bronson would send everyone off with apples from his orchard.

During the day, when Lu wasn't doing housework, she spent much of her time "sewing violently" by hand and knitting. She worked hard trying to make nice, hand-stitched summer clothes for her sister May. "She sent for me to make and mend and buy and send her (an) outfit," Lu wrote. But when Lu's older sister, Anna, learned that Lu was wearing the old clothes that she and May had left behind, Lu's sisters pooled their money and sent her a new dress to wear. "The great parcel, with a loving letter, came to me as a beautiful surprise," Lu noted.

In addition to making clothes for her family, Lu joined the women in Concord in their organized sewing bees. "Spent our May-day working for our men," Lu recorded. "Three hundred women all sewing together in the hall for two days." At the start of the Civil War the government was unable to provide enough clothing, food, shelter, and health care for the soldiers, which created a tremendous demand for uniforms, blankets, tents, and bandages. It was up to the soldiers' families and community to provide what the government couldn't. So women came together to form local Soldiers' Aid Societies, organizing sewing bees, lint picks (scraping piles of lint off material, which was used to pack wounds), fund-raisers, and food and supply drives. Joining a Soldiers' Aid Society was the socially acceptable and extremely valuable way for women to participate in the war. But for Lu, it wasn't enough. She wanted to do more.

By the end of the year, Lu was able to turn her attention to her writing, but she was restless. "Wrote, read, sewed, and wanted something to do," Lu penned in her journal. One of the pieces Lu was working on was called "How I Went Out to Service." It was a story about her bad experience working as a domestic servant. She sent it to the *Atlantic Monthly*, but the new publisher, James Fields, who was married to her distant cousin, rejected it, and told her to "stick to your teaching; you can't write." Lu understood that rejection was part of the publishing process, but she also understood that female writers didn't garner the same respect, status, and prestige as their male counterparts. Publishers and critics didn't consider women's literary works as "significant or as worthy." Successful female writers were criticized for being opinionated and scholarly, and stereotyped as "brainy, selfish, unladylike, and unattractive."

Despite Fields's harsh words, Lu wasn't going to give up. "Being willful, I said, 'I won't teach; and I can write, and I'll prove it." Fields told Lu that he had more manuscripts than he could publish, and he was choosing the war stories to "suit the times." "I will write 'great guns' Hail Columbia & Concord fight, if he'll only take it," Lu wrote. "For money is the staff of life & without, one falls flat no matter how much genius he may carry."

First she needed to focus on making some fast money to pay the bills. Lu didn't want to spiral down too far into financial despair. When Lu was twenty-five, the financial burden of caring for her family had almost overwhelmed her. She had no job prospects in sight, and Lu thought about jumping off a bridge to her death. "Last week was a busy, anxious time, & my courage most gave out," Lu told her family in a letter in October 1858. "For every one was so busy, & cared so little whether I got work or jumped into the river that I thought seriously of doing the latter. In fact did go over the Mill Dam & look at the water. But it seemed so mean to turn & run away before the battle was over that I went home, set my teeth & vowed I'd *make* things work in spite of the world." Luckily, Lu soon found work as a governess, much to the relief of her worried family. But she was left wary of ever reaching that point again.

So, in January 1862, when Elizabeth Peabody, a family friend who ran a successful school in Boston, asked Lu to open a kindergarten and James Fields encouraged her by offering a loan of forty dollars to set it up, Lu accepted. "Miss Peabody has opened a 'Kinder Garten.'... She has more babes than she wants...as it's hard times for story writers [I] shall be glad to lay hold of a few hundred in this way. Miss P expects to make $2,000 this year & if I can pick up a quarter of that I shall be contented," Lu explained.

Sadly, within a month, Lu was miserable with her new situation. "Very tired of this wandering life and distasteful work; but kept my word and tugged on....I never knew before...what false positions poverty can push one into," Lu noted. By May, the school had failed, and Louisa was in debt. "I gave it up, as I could do much better at something else....I wrote a story which made more than all my months of teaching...a wasted winter and a debt of $40—to be paid if I sell my hair to do it," Lu wrote.

During the summer of 1862 Lu turned her attention back to her writing and sent her stories to newspaper mogul Frank Leslie, the publisher of *Frank Leslie's Illustrated Newspaper*, which wasn't considered highbrow like the *Atlantic*. Leslie knew that women readers enjoyed sensational thrillers, so he gave them what they wanted to read—thrilling tales full of passion, jealousy, and revenge.

"Though my tales are silly," Lu described in her journal, "they are not bad; and my sinners always have a good spot somewhere. . . . Mr. L[eslie] says my tales are so 'dramatic, vivid, and full of plot,' they are just what he wants." Besides her family and close friends, few people knew Lu wrote what she called her "blood and thunder" tales. It was looked down on and not respectable, but she chose to write the tales because she could write them quickly. "They are easier to 'compoze' & are better paid than moral and elaborate works of Shakespeare," she confessed to her friend Alf Whitman (no relation to Walt). "So don't be shocked if I send you a paper containing a picture of Indians, pirates, wolves, bears & distressed damsels in a grand tableau over a title like this 'The Maniac Bride' or 'The Bath of Blood.' A thrilling tale of passion."

Lu didn't use her real name for the byline. Instead, she either used the nom de plume A. M. Bernard or no name at all. Not only did she want to avoid shocking her neighbors, but Lu also knew from experience that it was better to let the editor think she was a man. "A dozen [stories] a month were easily turned off, and well paid for," she recounted, "especially while a certain editor labored under the delusion that the writer was a man. The moment the truth was known the price was lowered; but the girl had learned the worth of her wares, and would not write for less, so continued to earn her fair wages in spite of sex."

Lu's thrillers tapped into her flair for the dramatic. Ever since she was a child, Lu liked to write and act in plays with her sisters and friends. "Louisa and her sister Annie [Anna] . . . were excellent actresses, and always in demand when private theatricals were on foot," as Frank Stearns, a friend and student at Sanborn's school, described them. "To see them perform . . . was a treat in the first order....Her acting had this peculiarity, that she seemed to always be herself and the character she was representing at the same time." Edward Emerson agreed, writing that Louisa had "a great taste for acting and skill in devising and producing wonderful romantic plays....Love, despair, witchcraft, villainy, fairy intervention, triumphant right, held sway in turn."

In the fall of 1862, Louisa was still busy sewing uniforms for soldiers and writing. "Sewing Bees and Lint Picks for 'our boys' kept us busy...wrote much...and sent it to L[eslie]., who wants more than I can send him. So, between blue flannel jackets for 'our boys'...I reel off my 'thrilling' tales....War news bad....I like the stir in the air, and long for battle like a warhorse when he smells powder. The blood of the Mays is up!" Lu wrote. Lu wasn't satisfied staying home and writing thrilling tales of adventure or sewing uniforms. She wanted to do her duty, but she wanted to live a life of adventure beyond what was deemed acceptable for a woman in serving a greater cause. She knew that if she had the opportunity to go out into the world, the life experience would help her develop as a person and writer, which, in turn, would allow her to further a cause that she passionately believed in while, at the same time, enabling her to take care of her family. Soon after the war broke out, Lu came up with a plan.

She'd been studying William Home's report on gunshot wounds as well as Florence Nightingale's recently published best-selling book *Notes on Nursing: What It Is and What It Is Not*. In 1862, the nursing profession was still in its infancy. Most nursing duties were assigned to men, soldiers recovering from injuries, because it was generally accepted that women were too fragile to cope with the demands.

In a letter to the editor of the *American Medical Times*, an Army surgeon voiced this belief:

Our women appear to have become almost wild on the subject of hospital nursing.... They, with the best of intentions in the world, are frequently a useless annoyance.... Imagine a delicate, refined woman assisting a rough soldier... supplying him with a bed-pan, or adjusting knots on a T-bandage employed in retaining a catheter in position.... Besides this, women as a rule, have not the physical strength necessary.... Women, in our humble opinion, are utterly and decidedly unfit for such service.

At the start of the war, the Union army barely had a medical department and lacked a system for distributing food, medicines, and supplies. In response to this, Elizabeth Blackwell, America's first female physician, organized the Women's Central Association for Relief in New York City. She and a number of male physicians, along with similar relief organizations, petitioned the government to establish a central relief organization called the US Sanitary Commission to distribute the supplies that the women made, the money they raised and to provide nurses for the battlefields and hospitals. The Sanitary Commission would also act as an advisory body to the Union army's medical department and keep tabs on the army's health conditions.

When the idea was brought before Surgeon General Clement Finley, he dismissed it as "a monument of weak enthusiasts and of well-meaning but weak silly women." Nevertheless, he reluctantly agreed to it so long as "the operations of the Commission should be confined to the volunteers," and the Sanitary

Commission, considered the forerunner to the American Red Cross, was established in June 1861.

Not long after the organization was established, an Alcott family friend, Dorothea Dix, who was a well-known mental health advocate and one-time teaching assistant to Bronson, was officially appointed superintendent of female nurses of the Union army, with a mandate to recruit female nurses. The announcement from the surgeon general's office in the War Department, which was publicized in newspapers, read, "Miss Dix has been entrusted by the War Department with the duty of selecting women nurses and assigning them to general or permanent military hospitals.... Women wishing employment as nurses must apply to Miss Dix or to her authorized agents."

Although she didn't have a nursing background, Dix was compared to Florence Nightingale "in her ministerings to the afflicted.... Her presence of supervision guarantees that all that can be done for suffering humanity will assuredly be done." At fifty-nine years old, the unmarried Dix had been tireless for the past twenty years in her one-woman crusade to improve the living conditions in hospitals for the mentally ill. Despite her poor health from a bout with malaria, she was stern, with a no-nonsense approach that didn't always win her friends, but it did earn her the nickname "Dragon Dix."

Despite the Union army's desperate need for nurses, which was made shockingly evident after its disastrous defeat in the Battle of Bull Run on July 21, 1861, Dix's first order of business was setting forth the requirements that women had to meet if they wanted to become army nurses—no exceptions. Dix didn't want nurses who were looking for husbands. So the applicants had to be at least thirty years old but no older than fifty, plain looking, and wear only brown, gray, or black clothing. Hoop skirts, which were very fashionable, were forbidden. Prerequisites included "habits of neatness, order, sobriety, and industry" along with two letters of recommendation "testifying to morality, integrity, seriousness, and capacity for the care of the sick." Free black women, regardless of class and education, were not considered for any nursing positions at this point in the war—with one exception. Sometimes they were allowed to nurse highly infectious white patients, especially if there was an outbreak of smallpox. Although surgeons and administrators did hire black women to work in all-white hospitals, they were assigned the menial jobs, such as cooking, doing laundry, emptying chamber pots, and washing floors.

Dix's regulations did not require a nursing education or any training because nursing schools didn't yet exist. The pay was $12.17 a month (men earned $20.50 a month), plus room and board, and a free round-trip train ticket. The length of service was six months or the duration of the war, whichever was shorter.

Lu would turn thirty on November 29, and as soon as she was old enough, she sent in her application. "I want new experiences, and am sure to get 'em if I go," Lu wrote in her journal. "So I've sent in my name, and bide my time writing tales, to leave all snug behind me, and mending up my old clothes—for nurses don't need nice things, thank Heaven!"

Chapter 3

A SOLDIER'S STORY

October 6, 1862, near Sharpsburg, Maryland
About two months before Lu enlists as an army nurse

O N OCTOBER 6, 1862, A FLAME OF LIGHT FLICKERED IN
the darkness of the cool night. John Suhre, a twenty-year-old Union soldier and blacksmith from Somerset County, Pennsylvania, was writing a letter to his sister. His tent was pitched one mile outside of Sharpsburg, Maryland, on Shepherdstown Road, among the gentle, rolling hills of green farmland and yellow cornfields that were now stained red with the blood of thousands of wounded and dead soldiers in the war's deadliest one-day battle.

John confided in his sister that he was homesick and worried. He didn't write about any fear of battle, injury, or death. Instead, John was feeling anxious because he hadn't received any letters from his family in three weeks.

The stamps that his fourteen-year-old brother, George, had sent him earlier had arrived safely. Despite the difficulty that all soldiers had keeping paper and stamps dry, John had written and mailed two letters home, one to his mother and one to his older half sister, Anna. John wanted to write also to his older half brother Emanuel, but he wasn't sure where to send the letter. Emanuel, who had been a printer's apprentice and a teacher, was now working and putting himself through Bethany College in Virginia. John's outspoken brother dreamed of one day being the editor and owner of a newspaper. Emanuel was also engaged to be married to Phoebe Colborn, a schoolteacher in Somerset, who was described as "a lady of culture and fine literary taste." Since John hadn't received any mail lately, he didn't know the details of Emanuel and Phoebe's wedding, which had taken place two weeks ago.

Consequently, John was left wondering whether his family had received any of his letters. His main worry was that he'd been paid twenty-seven dollars for his service in the army, which began on August 14, and, even though his family was relying on him for money, he was afraid that if he mailed it to them, they wouldn't receive it. So, he decided to keep the money for now.

John's family had experienced their fair share of financial hardship. In 1847, when John was five years old, he was startled awake in the middle of the night as red-hot embers crashed down from the ceiling. The house his family lived in at Critchfield's Mill was ablaze. Fortunately, his family slept on the first floor and woke up in time to get out. But they lost nearly everything in the fast-burning fire, which was later blamed on the stovepipe.

His father, Joseph, was a German immigrant who had come to America and found work as a miller in the wooded highlands of Somerset County. It was there that he met John's mother, Sarah, who, at the time, was in her midthirties and a recent widow with five children. They married in 1840, and John was born the following year. Joseph and Sarah had two more children together, and, throughout the years, they made their home in the various small villages, including Elk Lick and Milford, that made up Somerset County. But a few years prior to the war, his father died, and their mother, who was now in her midfifties, was struggling to make ends meet.

When the war began and President Lincoln called for volunteers, John's older half brother Mike enlisted, joining the Thirty-Ninth Regiment of the Tenth Pennsylvania Reserves, Company A, on June 20, 1861. One year later, Mike was wounded and taken prisoner at the Battle of Gaines's Mill, a bloody victory for the shrewd and strategic Confederate general Robert E. Lee. By the following month, Mike was paroled and recovering in a war hospital. Although he planned on returning to the Union army as soon as he could, Mike hadn't been paid in five months. So John had sent him a dollar, explaining to his sister via letter, "I told him if he needed any more he should let me know. It is not very pleasant to be out of money altogether."

Despite his brother's plight, a month after Mike was admitted to the war hospital, John joined the Union army himself, signing on for nine months with the 133rd Pennsylvania Volunteers Regiment, Company D. Everyone in his company had been recruited from Somerset County. Major Edward Schrock was the commander, and Edward's younger brother, Amos, was the captain of the regiment.

For the nearly two months that John had been in the Union army, luck seemed to be on his side. Taller than the average soldier and handsome with brown hair, a beard, and serene eyes, John was well liked in his regiment, not only for his courage and physical strength but also for his thoughtfulness toward others. John was trained for combat at Camp Curtin in Harrisburg, near the State Capitol building. Afterward, his regiment was sent to Washington, DC, where they were brigaded with other volunteer regiments from Pennsylvania. They were then ordered to go to Alexandria, Virginia, where they established a camp for a few days until August 30, before grabbing their guns and charging toward the front where the Second Battle of Bull Run was taking place.

In an offensive attack, General Lee marched his fast-moving army within thirty-five miles of Washington, DC, where Union troops were waiting for their reinforcements. Even though Lee knew he was already outnumbered, better leadership and a higher morale among his soldiers helped them crush the Union army in a bloody three-day battle, resulting in 22,177 casualties. The Confederate victory in Virginia opened the door for the next invasion—Maryland, with their sights set squarely on Pennsylvania.

John and his regiment didn't fight in the Second Battle of Bull Run. It was over before they received the order. Instead, for the next two weeks, they dug entrenchments and were assigned to picket duty, guarding the army's encampment from possible enemy advancement and putting them at the highest risk of being the first to be wounded, killed, or captured.

On September 12, 1862, John and his regiment packed up their camp and traveled to Washington, DC, where they exchanged their weapons for Springfield muskets and sixty rounds of ammunition. With their new weapons in hand, they were ordered to protect the town of Frederick, Maryland, from falling into the grip of the Confederate army.

But after arriving in Frederick, on September 17, they were ordered to march twenty-three miles to Sharpsburg, Maryland, to fight in the Battle of Antietam, which had started early that morning. John and his regiment marched all night, but by the time they arrived the next morning, with tired and aching feet, the bloody battle was over.

Although it was a victory for the Union army because they had successfully stopped the Confederates from invading the North, Lincoln had wanted General George McClellan to destroy the rebel army and put an end to the war. But McClellan had been overly cautious and worried that he was outnumbered. While he was planning his next move, Lee and his army had enough time to retreat to safety. McClellan decided not to pursue the rebels.

The one-day battle had been a shocking bloodbath, leaving 23,000 dead and wounded. In the short time that John had been in the army, the number of casualties in the war was nearly two times the population of Somerset County. "The dead are strewn so thickly that as you ride over it [the field] you cannot guide your horse's steps too carefully. Pale and bloody faces are everywhere upturned. They are sad and terrible; but there is nothing which makes one's heart beat so quickly as the imploring look of sorely wounded men, who beckon wearily for help which you cannot stay to give," an eyewitness reported.

At the start of the battle, the Union army field surgeons were in desperate need of supplies, but the army's medical supply wagons were not due to arrive anytime soon. The doctors were forced to use corn husks to dress the wounds of the soldiers until Clara Barton, a volunteer nurse, unexpectedly showed up with a wagonload of bandages and medical supplies that she had spent the past year collecting. In her bonnet, red bow, and dark-colored skirt, Clara worked side-by-side with the field doctors. Bullets flew by, and one tore a hole through her sleeve and killed the soldier she was helping. Undaunted, Clara worked nonstop for two days, prompting James Dunn, a surgeon at Antietam, to say, "In my feeble estimation, General McClellan, with all his laurels, sinks into insignificance beside the true heroine of the age, the angel of the battlefield."

BACK IN Washington, five days after the slaughter in Antietam, Lincoln called a meeting with his cabinet members, which included Edwin Stanton, William Seward, and Salmon Chase. "I have, as you are aware, thought a great deal about the relation of this war to Slavery.... I think the time has come now.... The action of the army against the rebels has not been quite what I should have best liked. But they have been driven out of Maryland, and Pennsylvania is no longer in danger of invasion.... I made the promise to myself, and (hesitating a little)—to my Maker...and I am going to fulfill that promise," Lincoln said to them. He then issued the preliminary Emancipation Proclamation on September 22, declaring that on January 1, 1863, all slaves in the Confederate states "shall be...forever free."

In John's letter to his sister, he didn't mention that President Lincoln had visited the town of Frederick just two days prior. Although Lincoln hadn't prepared a speech, thinking it wasn't proper to make one, at this time, he did say to the military men, "I return thanks to our soldiers for the good service they have rendered...the hardships they have endured, and the blood so nobly shed for this Union of ours. I also return thanks...to the good men, women, and children in this land of ours for their devotion to this glorious cause.... May our children and children's children for a thousand generations continue to enjoy the benefits conferred upon us by our united country."

Lincoln also visited the battlefield of Antietam and met with McClellan, which sparked speculation that McClellan was going to be fired. "As yet, no one except his constitutional advisors know the purpose of his visit.... So far as we know, there have been no changes among the generals in the field. All is quiet," the *Alexandria Gazette* reported.

So, while the Union and Confederate armies regrouped and planned their next moves, John and his regiment settled into their Sharpsburg camp and prepared for the next battle. John didn't know how long they would remain there, but he asked his sister to send him one of their mother's old quilts. The nights were cold and "it would add to my comfort," he wrote. He ended his letter by asking her, "Give my love [to] Mother and all the rest and Remember your Devoted, John F. Suhre." After writing down his return address, John extinguished the flickering flame, unaware that he would soon be in the biggest fight of his life—with Lu by his side.

Chapter 4

HELP WANTED

Early December 1862, Concord, Massachusetts

"I AM GETTING READY TO GO TO WASHINGTON AS AN ARMY nurse in one of the Hospitals & expect to have a hard winter if I do," Lu wrote in a letter to her friend. "But I like it & want to help if I can.... If I was only a boy I'd march off tomorrow." While Lu was waiting on pins and needles to receive a letter detailing her nursing assignment, she spent the first week of December washing, sewing, and mending her clothes. "I reviewed every rag I possessed," Lu wrote. "I detailed some for picket duty while airing over the fence; some to the sanitary influences of the washtub; others to mount guard in the trunk; while the weak and wounded went to the Work-basket Hospital, to be made ready for active service again."

When she was finished with her tasks, time seemed to slow down even more, and she felt "powerfully impatient" as her life in Concord went on as usual. "Father writing & talking, taking care of the schools & keeping his topsy turvy family in order," Lu detailed. "Mother sings away among her pots & pans, feeds & clothes all the beggars that come along, sews for the soldiers & delivers lectures on Anti slavery & Peace wherever she goes. Annie [Anna, Lu's older sister] & and her good man John…hope to have a little Lu [a baby]….I write stories, help keep house…Abby [May, Lu's younger sister] teaches drawing & music, goes to parties, rides horseback, rows boats, has beaux & is a…pretty girl."

Lu's younger sister, twenty-one-year-old Abigail, who preferred to go by the name May, was back from Syracuse and now teaching at Frank Sanborn's school. With May's return home, their next-door neighbor, Julian Hawthorne, stopped by the Alcotts' house every chance he had, usually on his walk to and from school. Although sixteen-year-old Julian was several years younger than May, he'd been in love with her from the moment he first spoke to her, which was two years prior, right after his family moved in next door. They were standing on the path at the bottom of the hill between their homes when May started the conversation by asking her bashful neighbor, "Do you like ladies and gentlemen bathing together?"

Julian was shocked, recalling, "My conceptions of bathing had till then been confined to the severe isolation of bathrooms, or to hardly less unsocial English sea beaches, where the sexes were rigorously segregated….I glanced at Abby's [May's] well-turned figure, her clustered yellow ringlets, her cheerful and inviting expression….I stammered, blushed."

May explained to him, "We and the Emersons often go over to Walden [Pond in] this hot weather to the cove where Thoreau used to live; there's a tent for the girls. We're going next Thursday; you could have John's bathing dress; It would be awfully nice!"

Julian couldn't remember the rest of the conversation, but he would never forget swimming at Walden Pond. Except for

Lu, who let her long hair down, everyone was wrapped like mummies, from head to ankle, bobbing up and down in their dark-blue flannel swimming suits. "The Alcott girls were society in themselves and Concord would have been crippled without them," Julian recounted. "Anne [Anna], when she could be spared from her own married sphere, was a precious element; Abby's [May's] enjoyment gave to others; and Louisa was the hub of the little universe and kept the wheel in constant activity."

Lu tried to stay busy to combat her feelings of restlessness while she waited each day for the mail to arrive. She continued to do whatever she could from the sidelines to help the soldiers. When she found out that a care package was being sent to some of the soldiers from Concord, Lu quickly filled two bags with nuts and apples for her dear "Old Boys," Edward "Ned" Bartlett and Garth Wilkinson "Wilkie" James.

Ned and Wilkie had been students at Frank Sanborn's school, and although they were only seventeen years old, they decided to quit school to join the Forty-Fourth Regiment of the Massachusetts Volunteers. Ned was the son of Concord's doctor, Josiah Bartlett. Although Dr. Bartlett treated both rich and poor and always made house calls no matter the time, distance, or weather, he wasn't always popular with the townsfolk. Dr. Bartlett was the founder of Concord's Total Abstinence Society, and his crusade against drinking resulted in his apple trees getting girdled so they'd die, his horse's tail getting cut, and the roof of his buggy getting slashed.

Despite his father's unpopular stance with the tavern keepers and farmers, both Ned and Wilkie were sorely missed, especially at the social gatherings. Wilkie, who was known for wearing the widest peg-top trousers and a muffin-shaped hat, was the most popular and fashionable at school. "Wilkie was incomparable," Julian, who was his schoolmate, wrote. "Besides the best dressed boy in the school, and in manners and talk the most engaging, his good humor was inexhaustible." Wilkie was the third son of the wealthy and prominent James family. His older brother, Henry, an aspiring novelist, was away at Harvard University, devouring Hawthorne's *The Scarlett Letter* and *The House of Seven Gables*. Unlike his older brother, Wilkie preferred action to studying, and he wanted to fight for his ideals. "I had been brought up in the belief that slavery was a monstrous wrong, its destruction worthy of a man's best effort, even unto the laying down of life," Wilkie said.

Since joining the Union army in August, Wilkie and Ned had already fought in the Battle of Rawl's Mill in North Carolina, driving back the Confederate soldiers. But the surprise attack from the rebels had been a trying ordeal for their inexperienced regiment, which had only been together for sixty days.

So the care package from home, which was to be sent for their "jollification & comfort" would, no doubt, be greatly appreciated. Along with the apples and nuts, Lu enclosed a letter: "Ned! Your sisters say you like apple sauce so I beg you'll have as many messes as you like out of the apples that grew in the old trees by the straw-berry bed where Wilkie stood one day with his hands in his pockets while we fed him with berries till he was moved to remark, with a luxurious condescension, 'hell this is rather a nice way of eating fruit isn't it?' You don't have time for that sort of amusement now, do you Sergeant?" Before signing off, she gave them some advice. "Now boys," Lu advised. "If you intend to be smashed in any way just put it off till I get to Washington to mend you up, for I have enlisted & am only waiting for my commission to appear as nurse at the 'Armory' Something Hospital, so be sure you are taken there, if your arms or legs fly away, some day (which the Lord forbid!) & we will have good times in spite of breakages & come out jolly under creditable circumstances."

A week after sending the care package, Lu's unbearable wait was finally over. On December 11, 1862, almost two weeks after her thirtieth birthday, Lu received a note in the mail from her friend Hannah Stevenson. An outspoken abolitionist like Lu and her family, Stevenson had helped Lu when she was at her lowest point of despair and was considering jumping from a bridge—it was Hannah Stevenson who had helped bring Lu from the brink by finding her work as a seamstress before the governess position was offered.

Shortly after the war began, fifty-three-year-old Stevenson was the first woman from Massachusetts to volunteer as a nurse. For the past year, she had worked in various Union hospitals. "The work is immensely hard, but I get used to it," Stevenson wrote to her family. "If we could do it as citizens, instead of soldiers, it would be easy." She found it especially difficult working with the doctors. "I cannot get over my surprise of being ordered about by these doctors as they order the privates," she explained further. "They recognize nothing of the peculiarity of the position; we have not been put under arrest yet, nor deprived of our rations, but scolded plentifully for not always obeying exactly minute contradictory orders. The army is an awful school in some respects, & few men have the self-control to use power well."

Stevenson also found Dix, the superintendent of female nurses for the Union army, very prickly, living up to her nickname, Dragon Dix. Dix had advised Stevenson "to be very careful, for you talk & laugh very loud and you talk a great deal. I want you to remember that you are nothing but a nurse &

to have nothing whatever, to say to Dr. Crosby." Stevenson and Crosby "had a great laugh over" this advice. The doctors didn't like Dix's authority over them in the hiring of female nurses, but they found a loophole when the assistant surgeon general, Dr. Robert Wood, told them, "Miss Dix has nothing to do with volunteer nurses...her work is to get nurses who are paid."

When Miss Dix discovered that the head doctor had allowed "volunteer" nurses in the newly converted and very crowded Union Hotel Hospital in Georgetown, she was furious that her authority had been challenged. Dix raged against the doctor and Stevenson, causing an unpaid nurse named Sarah Low to wonder how Stevenson could endure being spoken to in such a nasty way. "Miss Dix has always been very insolent to Miss S[tevenson]. She is arbitrary to them all. 'My nurses,' she calls them & does not look out for their comfort in the least. She wanted Miss Stevenson to send to Mass[achusetts] for one hundred nurses, but she would not because she knew they would not be treated decently if they came."

Unfortunately, Hannah Stevenson had become used to it.

Despite Dix's rants and raves, Stevenson was good at her job as the matron in charge of the Union Hotel Hospital, and her patients respected her. "They think so highly of Miss Stevenson, & well they may. It makes an immense difference to a soldier whether he gets into a hospital where there are women nurses or not, no one can tell how much, who has not lived in a hospital," Sarah Low wrote.

When Dix offered Stevenson a nursing position in a field hospital, however, she turned her down. She was suffering from neuralgia, rheumatism, and a toothache, and the pain fueled her worry that she might have to give up nursing. "My old ankle will give out every few days, and send me limping about, & to get off there, & find myself incompetent would be horrifying."

Stevenson was home on furlough when Lu received her letter calling her to report for duty as a nurse at the Union Hotel Hospital, where they desperately needed a nurse since she left. Lu was to be there in two days.

Although excited, Lu felt a pang of disappointment that she wouldn't be working at the Armory Square Hospital, in Washington, which was her first choice. The Armory was known to be one of the best, a benchmark for all the other hospitals, unlike the Union Hotel Hospital, which Lu knew was "a hard place." But her mind was made up. "Decided to go to Washington as nurse....Help needed and I love nursing, and *must* let out my pent-up energy in some new way. Winter is always a hard and a dull time, and if I am away there is one less to feed and warm and worry over," Lu recorded in her journal.

Her family and friends supported her decision. "The Civil War so kindled her that no one was astonished, or ventured to remonstrate, when she took the almost unheard decision to volunteer as (a) nurse behind the lines," her friend Julian wrote.

Lu only had a few hours to get ready if she was to make the train to Boston, the first leg of her journey. Although she had her clothes picked out, Lu needed to write her name in them, and she also needed to pack—there was too much to be done in the short window of time.

Lu's mother rushed next door to the Hawthornes' home for help. Although Julian was a fixture at the Alcotts' home, they rarely saw his father, Nathaniel. He was a shy man, and he didn't care much for Bronson, especially when Bronson went on and on about the virtues of pears.

"You may begin at Plato or the day's news," Nathaniel said, "and he will come around to pears. He is now convinced...that pears exercise a more direct and ennobling influence on us than any other vegetable or fruit."

Although he hadn't been feeling well recently, Nathaniel was locked away in his library with the blinds pulled down, trying to write another best seller. Occasionally, Lu would see him leave the house.

"We catch glimpses of a dark mysterious looking man in a big hat and red slippers darting over the hills or skimming by as if he expected the house of Alcott were about to rush out and clutch him," Lu wrote.

But Lu's mother wasn't there to see Nathaniel. She was there to seek out Nathaniel's wife, Sophia, who had offered to help Lu in any way she could. It was a whirlwind of activity. Sophia was carefully writing Lu's name in her clothes, while Louisa and her family raced around trying to help her get ready. Along with her dark and drab dresses, Lu packed her hairbrush, books by Charles Dickens, games, a copper teakettle, and her inkstand. "I packed my 'go-abroady' possessions, tumbled the rest into two big boxes, danced on the lids till they shut...then I choked down a cup of tea, generously salted instead of sugared by some agitated relative," Lu wrote.

She was also given sandwiches, gingerbread, and pears for the long journey to Washington, DC. Julian and May offered to walk Lu to the train depot. By now, daylight had turned to twilight, and Lu was ready to go "to the very mouth of the war."

Wearing a big black bonnet, a fuzzy brown coat, and a brave face, Lu hugged her family. Her father felt like he was sending his only son off to war. Lu felt the same way. Maintaining her composure, Lu didn't shed a tear until she heard her mother let out a despairing sob. Lu felt her courage slip away, and doubt bubbled up inside her. Everyone was crying, including Lu. "I realized that I had taken my life in my hand, and might never see them all again," Lu wrote. She hugged her mother close and asked, "Shall I stay?"

Although Lu's mother had told Sophia that she would feel helpless without Lu, she pushed the thought aside. "No, go!" her mother said, clasping her wet handkerchief and smiling bravely. It was an answer that Abba would later regret.

Chapter 5

GEORGETOWN OR BUST

One day later, December 12, 1862
On the train to Washington, DC

IT WAS SEVEN O'CLOCK AT NIGHT. THE TRAIN WAS RUMBLING down the tracks, southward to New London, Connecticut, a port town that notorious traitor Benedict Arnold had looted and burned to the ground during the Revolutionary War. Once there, Lu planned on catching an overnight steamboat to Jersey City, where she would board another train.

Looking out the window, there was nothing to see but the dark night. Inside the passenger car, the gas lamps glowed. Lu was comfortable in her seat, but feelings of loneliness stirred. She reached into her coat pocket for a piece of carefully wrapped gingerbread and the pear from home. She munched her food, trying to comfort herself.

Lu was worried about misplacing her ticket, so she had pinned it to the seat in front of her and was keeping a close eye on it. The free ticket hadn't been easy to obtain, and she'd spent the day running all over Boston trying to navigate the government bureaucracy.

A typical train ticket from Boston to Washington, DC, cost nearly twelve dollars, a whole month's salary for a female Army nurse and more than Lu's father made in a month as the superintendent of the Concord schools. So Lu was determined to procure the free ticket even though she needed to ask Ginery Twichell, the clean-shaven, ruddy-faced president of the Boston and Worcester Railroad company. "I'm a bashful individual, though I can't get any one to believe it," Lu confessed. "So it cost me a great effort to poke about the Worcester depot till the right door appeared, then walk into a room containing several gentlemen, and blunder out my request in a high state of stammer and blush."

Twichell, who first made a name for himself as a whip-fast stagecoach driver, was a self-made, shrewd businessman, with a seemingly endless supply of jokes. His competitive drive to be the first stagecoach driver to deliver a dispatch, which usually arrived at night, led him to sleep in his clothes with his buckskin underwear on. That way, he was not only ready to go but, during the long horse rides in the snowy, cold winter months, the buckskin underwear was advertised to give him the best "protection against pneumonia, rheumatism, and lung diseases." Despite Twichell's penchant for telling racy anecdotes, he was very courteous to Lu, but he had no idea what she was talking about. "It was evident that I had made as absurd a demand as if I had asked for the nose off his respectable face," Lu noted.

Speaking in a clear and low voice, Twichell, who had the nervous habit of briskly rubbing his hands together whenever he spoke in earnest, suggested that Lu talk to John Andrew, the governor of Massachusetts. Lu backed out of the room and soon found herself outside the Worcester depot on the corner of Lincoln and Beach Streets, across the muddy road from the grand United States Hotel.

Initially, Lu didn't think she had the nerve to pursue it any further. But Governor Andrew had a reputation for being genial and good natured, and Lu, who had lived in Boston, remembered seeing him once, eating oysters and laughing as if he didn't have a care in the world. She began walking toward the State House.

She passed through Boston Common, the seventy-five-acre, tree-lined public park where pirates and accused witches were once hanged from a large elm tree. For many years, people also used the Common for a cow pasture, which came in very handy for Lu's great-aunt Dorothy, who lived in a mansion across the street from the park, next to the State House.

Dorothy, who was married to Boston's one-time governor John Hancock, didn't have enough milk to serve the nearly two hundred French naval officers who arrived unexpectedly at her doorstep for breakfast one morning in 1778. She quickly sent her servants across the street to milk her neighbors' cows in the Common and told them that if anyone complained, she would explain everything to them. But no one did. Dorothy and John were popular with the people of Boston, and her husband had, after all, donated the wine and fireworks for the celebration in the Common when the Stamp Act was repealed in 1765.

When Lu finally reached the end of Boston Common, she was at the top of Beacon Hill, in front of the State House, which just happened to be built on the land that was once John Hancock's very own cow pasture. The brick, Federal-style building, with its row of imposing white pillars, was hard to miss. The shiny copper dome, which was made by silversmith Paul Revere, was like a beacon.

Lu climbed the mountain of steps and walked inside the State House, where she knocked on all the wrong doors, having no idea where to find the governor. "I turned desperate," Lu wrote. "And went into one, resolving not to come out till I'd made somebody hear and answer me."

The room was crowded with people, including soldiers and surgeons. Lu approached a man and asked whether he knew where she could find the governor or whether he knew anything about the free train passes for nurses. He said he didn't, but she had him cornered and continued prodding the "animated wet blanket" until he finally remembered that there was a sergeant somewhere on Milk Street in the financial district who might be able to help her.

Lu made her way to Milk Street, where she asked a gentleman who was passing by where she might find the elusive sergeant who knew about the free train pass. He didn't know, so she asked several more people before one suggested she look for the sergeant in Haymarket Square, near Faneuil Hall.

Lu raced to the open-air market, crossing more muddy roads, her shoes and the hem of her dress becoming caked with mud. She looked hard for a posted sign, stopped in shops and asked storekeepers, and even went into a restaurant, where women weren't supposed to go alone, and stopped by a recruiting tent. No one seemed to know or want to help her until she happened to run into her brother-in-law, John Pratt. She hurriedly told him her troubles. "I'm going to Washington at five, and I can't find the free ticket man....I'm so tired and cross I don't know what to do," Lu said.

Then she asked him for his help even though she would later explain, "I'm a woman's rights woman, and if any man had offered help in the morning, I should have condescendingly refused it, sure that I could do everything as well, if not better myself. My strong-mindedness had rather abated since then, and I was now quite ready to be a 'timid trembler,' if necessary."

John thought he knew someone nearby who could help, and soon Lu was standing in front of someone who knew about the free travel pass to Washington, DC. Lu thought her troubles were over, but she was wrong. She was told that she needed to obtain the order from someone over on Temple Place, a side street back near the Common. So she ran across the Common for a second time and finally got the order with carefully written directions outlining which trains she could take to the capital. She then ran back to Haymarket Square to present the paperwork to a young man. The young man took his time, looking out the window, eating peanuts, and gossiping with his colleagues. "I don't imagine he knew the anguish he was inflicting," Lu wrote. "For it was nearly three, the train left at five, and I had my ticket to get, my dinner to eat, my blessed sister to see, and the depot to reach, if I didn't die of apoplexy."

Twenty minutes later, a boy of no more than sixteen gave her the stamped and verified documents with careful instructions to go to a steamboat office for the train tickets. Lu wasn't sure why the train tickets would be at a steamboat office, but she didn't bother to ask. She was waiting for the boy to tell her to look both ways before crossing the street and give her a pat on the head as if she were a child. Despite this, Lu finally had her hard-won documents. She hurried to the steamboat office.

"A fat, easy gentleman gave me several bits of paper, with coupons attached, with a warning not to separate them, which instantly inspired me with a yearning to pluck them apart, and see what came of it," Lu noted.

But instead, she clutched her tickets protectively and had a quick bite to eat before being whisked away in the train.

❦

LU GAZED at the train ticket that she had pinned on the seat in front of her. She was finished with her snack and wanted to find comfort in a good conversation. But as a woman traveling alone, she wasn't supposed to talk to any men on the journey, not even the seemingly respectable-looking one sitting next to her.

Women were warned to be cautious when traveling by themselves. In the book *A Manual of Etiquette with Hints of Politeness and Good Breeding*, Daisy Eyebright, a pseudonym for Sophia Orne Johnson, who was well acquainted with the members of society in Washington, DC, explained:

> Appearances are proverbially deceitful, and we cannot think it desirable for young ladies while traveling alone in cars or steamboats, to permit gentlemen of even the most respectable outward seeming to enter into social conversation with them. White hairs and old age may be allowed such favors sometimes, but we must council a reticent demeanor in young lady travelers. Elderly ladies can suit themselves about such matters.

Furthermore, if a man asked Lu any questions, she was to answer in monosyllables to discourage him from starting a conversation. But Lu wasn't interested in following the rules. "Having heard complaints of the absurd way in which American women become images of petrified propriety, if addressed by strangers, when traveling alone, the inborn perversity of my nature causes me to assume an entirely opposite style of deportment," Lu wrote.

So she turned to the man sitting in the seat next to her. "I put my bashfulness in my pocket, and plunge[d] into a long conversation on the war, the weather, music, Carlyle, skating, genius, hoops, and the immortality of the soul," Lu recalled.

When the train reached New London, it was nearly eleven o'clock. Lu gathered her things, held onto her travel documents, and allowed the gentleman sitting next to her to walk her to the ferry called *City of Boston*, which was considered the fastest steamboat on Long Island Sound. Lu hadn't been on a steamboat before, and she was painfully aware that she didn't know how to proceed. But then she overheard a woman say, "We must secure our berths at once." So Lu dashed into one in the ladies' section and slipped off her winter coat with its pockets still filled with gingerbread. She climbed onto her bed and pulled the curtains closed before eventually peeping back out.

Although the boat was new with elegant furnishings, Lu was concerned it would sink. "If it ever intends to blow up, spring a leak, catch afire, or be run into, it will do the deed tonight," Louisa worried, "because I'm here to fulfill my destiny."

Lu had experienced a lot of disappointment in her life and thought bad luck might thwart her. But she pushed the thought aside and replaced it with her unwavering determination. She removed her bonnet, hung it on a peg, and placed her bag and umbrella on a little shelf, thinking that a hoop skirt might help her stay afloat. "I've no intention of folding my hands and bubbling to death without an energetic splashing first," she wrote. Eventually, her fear gave way to a fitful sleep, and the next morning, at seven o'clock, she was sitting in another train, heading for Washington, DC. Everyone around her seemed to despise traveling, if the screaming children, fretting women, growling men, and swearing porters were any indication. The food Lu brought along from home didn't give her as much comfort this time. "Think that my sandwiches would be more relishing without so strong a flavor of napkin, and my gingerbread more easy of consumption if it had not been pulverized by being sat upon," Lu wrote.

Several hours later the train passed through Baltimore, and Lu was now forty miles and two and a half hours from her destination. Looking out the window, she saw the spot where the Baltimore Riot took place. Shortly after the start of the war, when Lincoln desperately needed soldiers to protect the capital from falling into Confederate hands, seven hundred volunteer soldiers from the Sixth Massachusetts Volunteer Militia boarded a train for DC. When they arrived in Baltimore, they had to get off the train and walk through Baltimore to a different depot to board another train.

As the Yankee soldiers walked through Baltimore, chaos erupted. Southern sympathizers threw bricks and stones, and the soldiers fired their weapons. Nine civilians and three soldiers were killed, and two dozen soldiers and an unknown number of civilians were wounded. It marked the first bitter bloodshed in the war, and, as Lu passed by, she felt as if she "should enjoy throwing a stone at somebody, hard."

Looking out the window, she saw evidence of the war everywhere. Soldiers routinely camped near the railroad tracks to guard against sabotage and to maintain access for the delivery of supplies. "A most interesting journey into a new world full of stirring sights and sounds, new adventures, and an evergrowing sense of the great task I had undertaken," Lu recounted in her journal. "I said my prayers as I went rushing through the country white with tents, all alive with patriotism, and already red with blood."

Turning away from the window, she focused her attention on an elderly man and his wife. Although his wife was fussy and cross, the man said, "Yes, me dear," trying to grant her every wish. "I quite warmed to the excellent man, and asked a question or two, as the only means of expressing my good will. He answered very civilly, but evidently hadn't been used to being addressed by strange women in public conveyances," Lu wrote. His red-nosed wife didn't like it, and she "fixed her green eyes upon me, as if she thought me a forward hussy," Lu wrote.

Soon after, Lu turned her attention back to the window. She noticed the landscape outside wasn't too different from home, just flatter and less wintery, but on the edges of the barren-looking fields, the Union soldiers, dressed in their blue uniforms, had set up camps. As the train rumbled past, the people waved their hats. Lu, who was accustomed to seeing free black leaders and people in the North, was surprised by the appearance of working slaves in Maryland.

"We often passed colored people," Lu noted. "Looking as if they had come out of a picture book, or off the stage, but not at all the sort of people I'd been accustomed to see at the North."

It was night by the time Lu arrived in Washington. She told the driver of the horse-drawn carriage parked outside the station that she was going to the Union Hotel Hospital, located on the corner of Bridge and Washington Streets. As they headed down Pennsylvania Avenue, she saw the White House lit up and carriages moving in and out of the gate. "Pennsylvania Avenue, with its bustle, lights, music, and military, made me feel as if I'd crossed the water and landed somewhere in Carnival time,"

Louisa wrote. She looked for the famous East Room where Lincoln met with all kinds of important and common people and where big social events were held. At the start of the war, it was also where Union soldiers slept, under the sparkling chandeliers and frescoed ceiling, while guarding the president, whose office was directly above them, from a possible invasion by Confederate soldiers.

THE SOLDIERS' boots had ruined the carpet, but it didn't matter. Lincoln's wife, Mary, was already busy with her plans to redecorate. She wanted the run-down White House, with its peeling wallpaper, torn curtains, threadbare carpets, and broken furniture, to be transformed into a showplace. When the press caught wind of Mary's extravagance while the country was waging war with soldiers suffering and dying, she was severely criticized in the papers. And when the bill arrived for the renovations, Lincoln balked. "I'll pay it out of my own pocket first—it would stink in the nostrils of the American people to have it said that the President of the United States had approved a bill overrunning an appropriation of $20,000 for *flub dubs* [trinkets] for this damned old house, when the soldiers cannot have blankets," Lincoln told Mary.

Less than a year after Mary undertook redecorating the White House, a funeral was held in the East Room for the Lincolns' beloved eleven-year-old son, Willie, who died on February 20, 1862, from typhoid. The doctor had tried everything to save him, treating him with Peruvian bark (quinine) and beef tea. "My poor boy," Lincoln said when he saw his dead son. "He was too good for this earth. God has called him home. I know that he is much better off in heaven, but then we loved him so. It is hard, hard to have him die!" Two white horses pulled the hearse, taking the small coffin to the Oak Hill Cemetery in Georgetown.

As THE driver of the carriage announced that they had arrived at the Union Hotel Hospital in Georgetown, Lu felt her heart start beating faster. She realized that she was now far away from home. But Lu tried to look dignified and walk boldly up the steps to the entrance, which was flanked by two guards. They tipped their hats and moved aside, allowing Lu to enter the hospital. "A solemn time, but I'm glad to live in it," Lu wrote in her journal. "And am sure it will do me good whether I come out alive or dead."

Chapter 6

BURNSIDE'S BLUNDER

December 13, 1862, Fredericksburg, Virginia

O N THE VERY DAY THAT LU WAS ON THE TRAIN TO Washington, DC, Union soldier John Suhre was about to fight in his first battle of the Civil War. He didn't know he was about to charge into a bloodbath.

For the past six weeks, John had survived the ever-changing tempestuous weather—relentless rain, snow, freezing winds—all while being told to hurry up and wait. He had marched nearly one hundred miles with wet feet through thick mud with no hope of a dry tent, warm blanket, or fire. The conditions were so miserable that one of his comrades joked he would gladly pay five dollars for the comfort of sleeping in a hog's pen.

Today, while John and his comrades waited for their orders in the unseasonably hot, summerlike weather, across the river, newly appointed Union general Ambrose Burnside was commanding the Army of the Potomac from his headquarters, a two-story brick mansion with magnificent views of Fredericksburg. It was a job Burnside never wanted, and his plans were going desperately wrong.

Burnside had been handpicked for the job after President Lincoln became frustrated with General George McClellan's overcautious nature and his refusal to go after Robert E. Lee's Confederate army at the Battle of Antietam. Lincoln wanted to end the war immediately. The war was nearing two years old, and he needed a military victory to silence his critics and bolster the Emancipation Proclamation, which he planned to sign at the start of the New Year. So Lincoln fired McClellan and replaced him with Ambrose Burnside.

Burnside had previously refused Lincoln's offer twice, aware of his own limitations. Nevertheless, his honesty impressed Lincoln, and on November 7 a courier showed up at Burnside's headquarters. He had traveled through a fierce blizzard with an important dispatch from the War Department. Inside the message read, "By direction of the President of the United States, it is ordered that Major-General McClellan be relieved from the command of the Army of the Potomac, and that Major-General Burnside take command of that army." It was an order, not an offer, and, when the startling news sunk in, Burnside wept. "The responsibility is so great," Burnside wrote to a friend, "That at times I tremble at the thought of assuming so large a command."

Although his size was imposing—Burnside was six feet tall with a barrel chest and bushy sideburns that grew into his moustache—he was known for his easy charm, honesty, and kindness. He had been born and raised on a farm in Indiana and was taught by a tenderhearted Quaker in a one-room schoolhouse. But the hard choices of war would reveal Burnside's darker side.

Burnside didn't grow up dreaming of becoming a soldier or general. As a young man, he was an apprentice to a tailor, eventually opening his own shop, until he realized that he didn't like it. So, he went to West Point to further his education, his only option at the time. It was there he met and befriended George McClellan.

After graduating, Burnside was a soldier in New Mexico, where he fought the Apaches, until an arrow pierced his neck. While recovering from his wound, he invented a carbine for guns that would help the cavalry load their weapons faster. The invention was so good, he received a patent and started a business. But shady dealings, which he was not privy to, ended up destroying it. McClellan offered him a place to stay and a job at the Illinois Railroad, where McClellan was president. It was while working at the Illinois Railroad that Burnside also became friends with the company's lawyer, Abraham Lincoln.

When the Civil War broke out, Burnside immediately offered his services, and he was appointed colonel in the Rhode Island militia. Following the First Battle of Bull Run, McClellan became commander of the Army of the Potomac, and Burnside was promoted to brigadier general. Burnside didn't let his friend down. He led a daring expedition to the North Carolina coast, effectively blocking any Confederate shipping, and was promoted to major general. But, at the Battle of Antietam, McClellan criticized Burnside for delaying his attack by ordering his troops to cross a bridge, creating a bottleneck, instead of wading across the water.

Nevertheless, Lincoln thought Burnside was the man for the job even though he was "the most distressed man in the army, openly saying he is not fit for the job."

McClellan tried to remain stoic when he heard the news that his friend was replacing him. "Poor Burn feels dreadfully, almost crazy—I am sorry for him, & he never showed himself a better man or truer friend than now," McClellan wrote to his wife. "Of course I was much surprised—but as I read the order...I am sure that not a muscle quivered nor was the slightest expression visible on my face....They have made a great mistake....I have done the best I could for my country....I have done my duty as I understand it. That I must have made many mistakes I cannot deny—I do not see any great blunders....Our consolation must be that we have tried to do what was right."

Within days of replacing McClellan, Burnside came up with a bold plan to capture Richmond, Virginia, the capital of the Confederacy, and crush the Confederate army. But it hinged entirely on speed and surprise. His enemy, Robert E. Lee, had his troops divided, with a week's march away from Fredericksburg, Virginia, a place that was best known as George Washington's hometown. Burnside's strategy was to march his troops nearly one hundred miles at a breakneck pace to Falmouth, Virginia, which was positioned along the bank of the Rappahannock River. Once there, they would build floating pontoon bridges to cross the river into Fredericksburg before Lee had any idea they were there. Unopposed, Burnside would lead his army into Richmond, which was thirty-five miles away.

He shared his plan with Lincoln, who thought it had promise. "The President has just assented to your plan. He thinks it will succeed if you move rapidly; otherwise not," General in Chief Henry Halleck telegrammed. Burnside successfully marched his troops, 65,000 men strong and including John Suhre, to Falmouth. But, once they were there, his plan started to unravel. The boats and supplies needed to build the pontoon bridges weren't

74

there. Poor communication and bad weather caused a ten-day delay. The element of surprise had vanished. While Burnside waited, and waited, General Lee consolidated his troops and fortified their position on higher ground, gaining an advantage and successfully blocking the road to Richmond.

Although the rebel soldiers were outnumbered, they waited patiently and with confidence. "A chicken could not live on the field when we open on it!" one exclaimed. Despite this, Burnside felt compelled to proceed with his flawed plan. The unyielding pressure and burden of ending the war was weighing heavily on him. When the supplies finally arrived, on December 11, he ordered his men to build the bridges. The rebel sharpshooters, who were strategically positioned in houses along the opposite side of the river, aimed and fired relentlessly, killing some of the men and delaying their effort even further. Burnside ordered the Union artillery to use their 150 cannons to bombard the city. "The bombardment was terrific and seemed ridiculously disproportionate to the enemy therein," one Union soldier wrote. "Like an elephant attacking a mosquito."

Clouds of black smoke rose from the city where nearly every house was damaged or destroyed by fire. Burnside then authorized the soldiers to cross the river in the pontoon boats and clear out the snipers hiding in the city. While the rebel sharpshooters continued to fire, Union soldiers hurriedly crossed the river in the unwieldly pontoon boats, paddling with their rifle butts. As soon as their feet touched the other side of the riverbank, they charged the rebel soldiers who were still standing strong. Street fighting ensued, the first of its kind in the Civil War, and the Confederate soldiers finally made a hasty retreat.

Once the city was secured, a group of Union soldiers went on a rampage, looting and vandalizing the abandoned homes and stores. An eyewitness reported:

[In] the old mansion of Douglas Gordon—perhaps the wealthiest citizen in the valley...every room had been torn with shot, and then all the elegant furniture and works of art broken and smashed....I found soldiers...diverting themselves with the rich dresses found in wardrobes, some had on bonnets of fashion of last year, and were surveying themselves before mirrors, which an hour or two afterward, were pitched out of windows and smashed to pieces upon the pavement; others had on elegant scarfs bound round their heads in the form of turbans, and shawls around their waists....Every store, I think without exception, was pillaged of every valuable article. A fine drug store...was literally one mass of broken glass and jars.

The looting wasted precious time and energy, and they would pay dearly for it.

With the city of Fredericksburg now in Burnside's hands, he assessed the Confederate's line of defense, seeing that they were positioned on higher ground in a semicircle. Burnside informed his officers that he was going to launch a frontal assault by attacking the right side first, followed by a full-on attack on the left side. His officers thought the plan was ill fated and spoke out. "The carrying out of your plan will be murder, not warfare," Colonel J. H. Taylor warned Burnside.

Burnside didn't listen. On December 13, he ordered a division of soldiers from Pennsylvania, which included John Suhre's recently reenlisted half brother, Mike, to spearhead the attack.

While John and his regiment waited anxiously in reserve, Mike and his division were ordered to charge an open field toward the densely wooded ridge on the right, called Prospect Hill, but it was soon renamed the "Slaughter Pen."

At first, the Confederate soldiers relentlessly fired their guns and cannons, but then they let the Union soldiers come within five hundred yards of the wooded area, where a fourteen-gun battalion was patiently waiting for them. For an hour, the battle raged, and the Union soldiers were able to break through the Confederate's line. But their success was short lived when Confederate reinforcements arrived, driving them back. "The action was close-handed and men fell like autumn leaves," one Union soldier said. "It seems miraculous that any of us escaped at all." John Suhre's half brother, Mike, wasn't one of them. He was killed in action.

The battle was far from over. At noon, Burnside ordered troops to storm Marye's Heights, on the left side. It was a suicide mission. Behind a stone wall on Marye's Heights, the Confederate soldiers were lined up in rows, with each row reinforcing the other. The soldiers in the back row loaded the weapons and handed them to the front. There was a steady hailstorm of bullets blazing at the Union soldiers, who were falling "like a steady dripping of rain from the eaves of a house."

Despite the loss of nearly 3,000 men in one hour, Burnside kept sending more and more troops to the stone wall, and the battle at Marye's Heights continued, causing one Confederate soldier to exclaim, "Ye Gods! It is no longer a battle, it is butchery."

It was brutal madness, and Burnside showed no mercy to his soldiers, refusing to give up. At 2:30 P.M., John Suhre's regiment was finally ordered to charge up the hill toward the stone wall.

John and his fellow soldiers dropped their knapsacks and held firmly onto their guns and bayonets, advancing toward their enemy with the pungent smell of gunfire smoke filling the air. After 250 yards, they came to a sudden halt and confusion erupted.

Lying before them, the dead and wounded blanketed the field. Some of the wounded men reached out and grabbed at their ankles, trying to stop John and his regiment from charging ahead. "Halt—lie down—you will all be killed," they warned. But John and his fellow soldiers were ordered to disregard them and keep charging forward to the enemy's line. They followed those orders, and some of them made it to within fifty yards of the stone wall at the crest of the hill. The Confederate soldiers behind the wall furiously fired their rifled muskets. "The stone wall was a sheet of flame," their commanding officer reported.

John and his surviving comrades finally dropped to the muddy ground, with nowhere to hide in the open field, forcing them to endure "a most terrific fire from the enemy's infantry and artillery."

They held their position for an hour while the sun began to set in the West, turning the sky and gun-smoked air a fiery red. Finally, night fell and darkness descended. Burnside had no choice but to withdraw and end the battle. It was a crushing defeat for the Union, and Burnside openly wept.

The field, which was dotted with remnants of the corn and wheat harvest, was now strewn with dead and wounded men, their blue uniforms stained with blood. The Union dead or injured were more than double that of the Confederates, with a toll of almost 13,000. John Suhre was one of them.

A bullet was lodged in his chest, another tore clean through his lung, and a third wounded his shoulder. John lay on the battlefield, listening to the screams of the wounded men. One witness described how "the cries of the wounded rose up over that bloody field like the wail of lost spirits all the night; cries for water, blankets and 'to be borne off the field'...terror and suffering...filled the very air with pain."

It would take nearly a week to remove the wounded from the battlefield. When they were finally cleared, Lu would be among those to receive them.

Chapter 7

THE HURLY-BURLY HOUSE

The next day, December 14, 1862,
Georgetown, Union Hotel Hospital

L U'S FIRST DAY AS A NURSE OFFICIALLY BEGAN AT 6:30 A.M. with the sound of reveille reverberating throughout the hospital. She lit a gas lamp, brightening her cheerless room.

In the too-small fireplace, a log crackled and spilled out onto the hearth. But the fireplace failed to make the room cozy. The broken windowpanes, which someone had draped with bedsheets, let the cold winter air creep in. A bottle of lavender water sat on the mantelpiece along with a candle without its candlestick, a flatiron to press her clothes, a shiny tin basin, and a copy of the Bible.

Lu crawled out of her narrow bed, pushing back the sheet, two blankets, and a coverlet marked with the words "U.S. Hosp. Dept." in indelible ink. The mattress and pillow were uncomfortably thin, and, like most beds in military hospitals, the bedframe was made of iron, which was believed to help prevent a bedbug infestation.

Stepping onto the cold floor, Lu tried not to trip over the burning log that was jutting out of the fireplace as she began to get ready in her sparsely furnished room. On the whitewashed wall, there was a pocket-sized mirror that hung over a tin basin with a blue pitcher for washing. She really couldn't see her reflection in the mirror, so Lu would have to make do. The hospital didn't have any washrooms with showers or bathtubs. However, it did have a few sinks and flushable toilets, but many of them didn't work. Inside her small closet, Lu had unpacked her plain-looking dresses, her big black bonnet, her bag, and her boots. The rest of her personal belongings were stored in a trunk behind the door.

Once dressed and her bed made, Lu was ready to start her day. Breakfast was served promptly at seven o'clock, and, as soon as the first bell rang, she could hear the thundering footsteps of the hospital staff. Lu joined the stampede, stepping into the narrow, twisting hallway and down two flights of stairs to join the twenty others sitting at the unpolished wooden table in the gloomy dining room.

The hospital wasn't at all what Lu expected or hoped for when she signed on to be a nurse far away in Concord. To her dismay, this hospital building, with its noticeably rotting woodwork and dirty wallpaper, had seen better days. The three-story brick building, built in 1796, had originally been a stylish hotel and tavern, featuring stables sufficient for fifty horses and numerous sheds for carriages. It had also boasted a robust spring of running water, located less than twenty yards from the kitchen, and a well-stocked bar of the best liquor. The once-fashionable hotel used to be a popular spot for wealthy plantation owners and prominent citizens. When John Adams became the second president of the United States, he stayed there while the White House was under construction. But, over the years, the hotel changed hands and fell into disrepair. Prior to the Civil War, the Union Hotel was a boardinghouse renting cheap rooms to clerks, teachers, and poor families. Soon after the war began, the government notified the proprietor that it was seizing the building under eminent domain and was converting it into a hospital to meet the overwhelming demand of wounded soldiers. The boarders were unceremoniously ordered to move out, so they packed up their belongings and took everything with them—including the chamber pots—making sure to leave nothing of value behind.

As Lu made her way through the converted hotel-hospital and entered the dining room, she learned that the stampede to the dining room was typical. No one wanted to be late to a meal; otherwise, there wouldn't be a crumb left to nibble on. This was surprising to Lu because she found the food almost inedible, bearing a striking resemblance to what she imagined prison fare to be like. The bread tasted like sawdust, the stewed blackberries looked like cockroaches, the coffee was muddy, and the huckleberry tea was weak and flavored with lime. Lu didn't trust the meat, but not because she was raised on a strict vegetarian diet. To her, the beef looked rotten, as if it had been around since the last war, and she suspected that the pork came from one of the many rowdy pigs that roamed freely through the muddy streets.

Although she made a mental note to go to the market and buy crackers, cheese, and apples to store in her room, Lu would later learn that this was a bad idea, owing to the unseen rats and bugs that were living in her closet. "I resigned myself to my fate, and remembering that bread was called the staff of life, leaned pretty exclusively upon it…varied by an occasional potato or surreptitious sip of milk," Lu wrote.

When the hospital staff was finished eating breakfast, the day shift began. The hospital matron, fifty-three-year-old Hannah Ropes, supervised the nurses, oversaw the washing and distribution of the clean clothes and bed linens, and made sure the soldiers received their meals. Despite Hannah's responsibility to manage the other nurses, the person who was in the position of power, and responsible for everyone and everything, was Dr. A. M. Clark, the "surgeon in charge." Female nurses were ranked low on the hierarchy, just above the cook and laundress, but beneath everyone else, including male nurses. But Hannah wasn't concerned about status. Nor was she concerned that the volatile Dix, whose headquarters were nearby and who dropped in on the hospitals, turned her nose up at her. Ropes didn't "care a fig" for Dragon Dix. Hannah Ropes had been working at the hospital since June 25 and had worked alongside Lu's friend, Hannah Stevenson.

Stevenson liked Ropes, calling her genial, cheery, wise, and sweet. But Ropes suffered from rheumatism, and sometimes the work was too physically demanding. "She is quite a feeble person for work so rough as this," Stevenson noted. "She seems like one who had somewhat been worn out with hard & uncommon exertions, & whose will is most self-sacrificing."

But during her tenure as the matron, Hannah Ropes proved she was a force to be reckoned with, causing some to shake in their army-issued boots. She had been born into a well-to-do family of prominent lawyers in Maine and Boston with political connections, but her independent spirit didn't always mesh with the traditional role that was expected of women at the time. She would have been headed toward what was then considered spinsterhood had she not married at the age of twenty-five. When her husband left her several years later, she risked her good reputation and standing in society by divorcing him.

Despite her failed marriage, Hannah embraced motherhood and was devoted to her children, Ned and Alice. But she was hungry for a higher purpose beyond the domestic sphere. "Why did you give this homely hen the wings of an eagle?" Hannah had once written to her beloved mother. "Behold they flap heavily against her sides, for want of proper use."

Hannah soon found her calling as an active abolitionist. When the Kansas-Nebraska Act was passed in 1854, allowing settlers to decide whether the new state of Kansas would be proslavery or free, Hannah packed up her belongings and moved her family from Boston to a log cabin there. She planned on spreading her antislavery ideas but found herself instead nursing her friends who were sick with malaria. The constant threat of violence between the proslavery and antislavery settlers, some of which was led by abolitionist John Brown, caused Hannah to keep "loaded pistols and a bowie-knife upon my table at night, (and) three Sharp's rifles, loaded, standing in the room."

She eventually moved back East where her antislavery beliefs were less dangerous. But her time there left a lasting impression, and Hannah wrote a book called *Six Months in Kansas*. She followed it up with a novel called *Cranston House*. The experience she gained caring for her sick friends in Kansas combined with reading Florence Nightingale's book further ignited her interest in becoming a nurse. And after the war, Hannah planned on writing a book about being a nurse at the Union Hotel Hospital.

Like many female nurses at the time, Hannah believed her role was to provide maternal kindness to the patients under her care. "I take the place of his mother at once," Hannah said about each individual soldier she treated. Her patients' welfare always came first. So Hannah sometimes had to ignore the hospital rules and chain of command, especially when she was dealing with a "jackal" like the new hospital steward, Henry Perkins.

When she discovered that Perkins, who was in charge of the supplies, was stealing the soldiers' clothes and rations and selling them for a profit, she told Dr. Clark. But Dr. Clark, who "walked around the ward with all the dignity of a lamp post," didn't do anything about it. "Between surgeons, stewards, nurses and waiters, the poor men in all the hospitals barely escape with life or clothes or money," Hannah revealed to her daughter, Alice.

Abusing sick and wounded soldiers wasn't just a problem at the Union Hotel Hospital; it was widespread. In September 1862, a special committee from various state relief associations reported their findings from a special investigation to the new surgeon general, William Hammond. The report harshly criticized the surgeons in charge of the Northern hospitals visited, many of the stewards, the nurses, and even the chaplains for "gross inattention, rudeness to philanthropic visitors, and frequent malappropriation of donated delicacies from the patients to their own benefit." The investigation also revealed how some of the hospital staff were stealing from the wounded and sick soldiers: "Food of the most miserable quality is served to the sick in some of the hospitals, and that the surgeons commute the full soldiers' rations which is the patients' due, and pocket the money themselves. It is believed that some of the most *unscrupulous clear a thousand dollars a month* by stealing the accruing hospital fund, keeping the sick and wounded in their charge on the meanest diet, and returning vouchers as of money applied to their comfort."

After the report was presented, Surgeon General Hammond promised to begin a vigorous investigation into the charges. So, when Dr. Clark failed to do anything about the steward, Hannah took it upon herself to write a letter to Hammond. She would eventually discover that despite his promise of "a vigorous investigation," he was not her ally.

"Surg[eon] Gen[eral] Hammond is said by those who have known him, to be a scheming ambitious man, & to be dead set against—women—nurses," Stevenson revealed.

Hammond's office did respond to Hannah's letter, but the letter was not addressed to her; it was sent to the head surgeon in charge of her. Again, Dr. Clark didn't do anything to the steward. Instead, he sent an "official notice" to Hannah telling her that she had to provide evidence.

"As though I had not better business to do than to dabble in such muddy water!" Hannah wrote in her journal. To Hannah, the evidence "was plain in the kitchen, in the larder, and every pinched face one meets in the stairs or in the wards."

But Hannah did find time to formally write back to Dr. Clark, stating:

How I came to judge him [the steward]...while contending with him for food suitable for the men, he said with a sneer he was not of the benevolent kind, that his business was to make all the money he could out of the hospital, adding triumphantly that the power was in his hands. If the sick privates had been dogs, he could not have spoken more contemptuously of them.

Not long after, Hannah found out that the steward had incarcerated a boy named Julius in a dark hole in the cellar, among the rats and cockroaches. Julius was a convalescing patient who had recovered enough to help in the hospital. Julius angered the steward when he sent too much food to one of the wards, and they came to blows. Julius filed a complaint with Dr. Clark, which the doctor ignored. Instead, Dr. Clark gave the steward orders to get Julius back to work, and if Julius refused, he was to be thrown by the neck and heels into a cell.

This time, Hannah went directly to Surgeon General Hammond's office, but he was too busy to see her. So, Hannah dashed off to his superior's office, the secretary of war, Edwin Stanton. It was no secret that Stanton didn't like Hammond.

Hannah had to wait only ten minutes before Stanton met with her. She spoke up, telling him about the black hole in the cellar.

"Call the Provost Marshall," Stanton said to his functionary. "Go to the Union Hospital with this lady, take the boy out of that black hole, go into it yourself so as to be able to tell me about it, then arrest the steward and take him to a cell in the Old Capital Prison, to await further orders!"

A few days later Dr. Clark was also arrested and sent to the Old Capital Prison. He was released after several days and later transferred out of the hospital. Before leaving, he confronted Hannah. But she refused to back down, telling him:

> If the thing should happen again of one of the patients brought here to recover, and you allowed the steward to throw him into that place, I should run for help. Why? Because I am a mother, and I have only to remember that each of these sick ones (has) a mother somewhere, and for the time, I act for them.

In fact, the wounded and sick soldiers reminded Hannah of her own son, Ned, who was a soldier in the Union army. Hannah worried about him constantly, and so did her daughter, Alice. Alice told Ned that if he got sick or hurt, to make sure he was taken to the Union Hospital so their mother could care for him.

"I wrote you all about her going," Alice wrote to her brother. "But suppose you have not received the letter. She likes the work very much and is doing a great deal of good."

Even though she had found her calling, Hannah discouraged Alice from visiting her at the hospital. "Now, it would not do for you to be here," she informed her daughter. "It is no place for young girls. The surgeons are young and look upon nurses as their natural prey....Wounded men are exposed from head to foot before the nurses and they object to anybody but an 'old mother.' This is not all. I don't like the tone of anything here. Refinement is not the order of society [of the hospital]."

REFINEMENT AT the Union Hotel was a thing of the past, which was evident when Lu walked into the ballroom on her first day. The once-glamorous room, noted for its Pompeian style mural, had been a destination for fancy balls, including one held in honor of George Washington. But the ballroom was now partitioned into patient wards containing iron beds lined up in neat rows and occupied with wounded and sick men from the Battle of Antietam and the Second Battle of Bull Run. Although the men had survived the battlefield, they now had to survive their stay at the hospital.

"The healing process is very slow," Hannah explained. "When they first come they appear to gain because we feed them and tend so well their wounds, but soon the suppuration takes place, lead has to be probed for, and then they get sad and lose their appetite."

Germ theory was not yet accepted in 1862. Although viruses and bacteria had been seen under a microscope, they were interpreted as part of the healing process, so doctors and nurses weren't aware that sterile conditions should be provided and maintained. However, it had also been observed, during the Revolutionary War, that wounded patients seemed to have a better chance of recovery if the hospital was uncrowded, clean, and well ventilated.

The first thing Lu noticed when she walked into the patient ward was the overpowering stench from the festering wounds and infection. The early rays of sun peeked through the closed windows while Lu watched a wounded man die. Afterward, she sat down on a hard chair and watched over a boy with pneumonia and a man who had been shot through the lungs. "I sat looking at the twenty strong faces as they looked back at me... hoping that I looked 'motherly' to them; for my thirty years made me feel old, and the suffering round me made me long to comfort every one," Lu later confided in her journal. The man with the chest wound just stared at Lu, not saying a word, and this made her nervous. When the boy sat up, gasping for breath, Lu placed her mother's little black shawl around his shoulders. He smiled at her and said, "You are real motherly, ma'am."

During the rest of her first day, she washed faces, served meals, and distributed medicine prescribed by Dr. George Stipp, who was the newly appointed chief. Considered a skilled surgeon (and a friend of President Lincoln's), Stipp was inclined to prescribe calomel, a medicine containing mercury, no matter what the ailment, believing it to be a cure-all. And, because more than half of the deaths at the hospital were caused not by gunshot wounds but by diseases such as typhoid, typhus, malaria, pneumonia, and smallpox, he was prescribing a great deal of calomel, which, like most medicines at the time, was useless and even harmful. Everyone, including Lu, was at risk.

"We get *lousy!* and dirty," Hannah wrote. "We run the gauntlet of disease from the disgusting *itch* to smallpox! My needle woman found nine body lice inside her flannel waistcoat after mending the clothes that had been washed! And I caught two inside the binding of my drawers!"

Looking around the decrepit ballroom, which had once been filled with music, dancing, and laughter, Lu noted that she was surrounded by "pneumonia on one side, diphtheria on the other, [and] five typhoids on the opposite." She knew that although she wasn't in the line of fire, she had the same chance of dying as the soldiers from the spread of disease. Even so, Lu worked from dawn until nine o'clock that night in a whirlwind of constant activity. "A strange day, but I did my best," Lu wrote. She would think of the Union Hotel Hospital as the "Hurly-Burly House."

Hannah was impressed with Lu's first day on the job: "We are cheered by the arrival of Miss Alcott from Concord—the prospect of a really good nurse, a gentlewoman who can do more than merely keep the patients from falling out of bed."

THREE DAYS later, on December 17, the wind was howling, and the rain was beating against the broken window when Lu was startled awake by a thundering knock on her door. "They've come, they've come!" someone was shouting.

Lu bolted upright in her bed. "Who have come?" she asked. "The rebels?"

"It's the wounded from Fredericksburg." Lu was told that she had fifteen minutes to get to the ballroom where the worst cases would be. "I am free to confess," Lu wrote, "that I had a realizing sense of the fact that my hospital bed was not a bed of roses just then." She sprang out of bed and hurried to the broken window, pulling the bedsheet-curtain back and looking out into the gray dawn light. She saw what looked like horse-drawn market carts lined up on the muddy street and watched them being unloaded until she realized they were ambulances filled with wounded soldiers. "My ardor experienced a sudden chill. And I indulged in a most unpatriotic wish that I was safe at home again."

Despite her misgivings, Lu quickly put on her dress, tied her pinafore, pinned up her long hair before covering it with a red scarf that identified her as a nurse, and slipped on her shoes. She made her way down the stairs and entered the main hall. Along with the din of clamoring voices and clattering footsteps, Lu was greeted with a sickening odor that hung in the air like a thick fog. The stench was overpowering, and Lu's only defense was arming herself with lavender water. She sprinkled some on her face, and, when that didn't work, she held the bottle under her nose.

Lu tried not to get in the way as the wounded men streamed into the crowded hospital. Some were on stretchers, some were being carried in other men's arms, and some were hobbling on makeshift crutches. "The hall was full of these wrecks of humanity," Lu wrote. "For the most exhausted could not reach a bed until duly ticketed, and registered; the walls were lined with rows of such as could sit, the floors covered with the more disabled."

Lu was surprised when the other nurses told her that these weren't even the worst cases. The more severely wounded were to arrive in a few days. After the fight at Fredericksburg, the fallen soldiers had been left on the battlefield for two nights while the enemy continued to fire their weapons, preventing anyone from helping them. The dead had been hastily buried where they fell. "The wounded are brought in, for the most part, over corduroy roads," one Union Hotel Hospital nurse wrote. "The suffering is indescribable. Often they are not able to keep to the direct road, but go first in one direction, then in another to escape the fire of guerillas [sic]."

Lu was overcome with emotion, but she quickly collected herself. "The sight of several stretchers, each with its legless, armless or desperately wounded occupant, entering the ward, admonished me that I was there to work, not to wonder or weep," Lu wrote. "So I corked up my feelings, and returned to the path of duty, which was rather 'a hard road to travel' just then." She took refuge behind some piles of clean shirts, socks, and bandages while she looked around the room. The wounded men, who were brought in from battle "with their clothes all on just as they were shot down," were covered with mud to their knees and wrapped with bloody bandages that hadn't been changed in days. She noticed that every one of them wore a look of defeat on his face. "I pitied them so much, I dared not speak to them, though remembering all they had been through . . . I yearned to serve the dreariest of them," Lu recalled.

Suddenly, she was yanked from her refuge by Julia Kendall, a nurse no "bigger than a pound of soap after a week's washing," who handed her a washtub, sponge, towels, and bar of brown soap. "Wash as fast as you can," Julia told Lu. "Tell them to take off socks, coats and shirts, scrub them well, put on clean shirts, and the attendants will finish them off, and lay them in bed." The men had to be bathed and checked for lice before they were assigned a bed.

Lu was shocked. "If she had requested me to shave them all, or dance a hornpipe on the stove funnel, I should have been less staggered." But she again "corked up" her feelings of apprehension and proceeded to do as Julia told her. "If I had come expecting to enjoy myself," Lu wrote to Hannah Stevenson, who was on furlough, "I should have paraded home again...as an all pervading bewilderment fell upon me the first few days, & when Miss Kendall calmly asked me to wash and put clean clothes on some eight or ten dreary faced, dirty & wounded men...I felt that the climax was reached & proceeded to do it very much as I should have attempted to cut off arms or legs if ordered to. Having no brothers & a womanly man for a father I find myself rather staggered...but...I still hope to get used to it & hold myself 'ready for a spring if anything turns up.'"

Lu held on tightly to the soap while she scanned the room. She noticed an older soldier with a bloody bandage around his head. His pants, socks, and shoes were plastered with thick mud. Lu offered to wash him. "He was so overpowered by the honor of having a lady wash him, as he expressed it, that he did nothing but roll up his eyes, and bless me, in an irresistible style which was too much for my sense of the ludicrous; so we laughed together," Lu noted.

When his clothes were set aside, they formed a mound of mud and would have to be taken to a small house out back and laundered in the clothes-boiler, a fifty-gallon cauldron attached to a furnace. In the meantime, Lu washed him and several others. "I took heart and scrubbed away like any tidy parent on a Saturday night. Some of them took the performance like sleepy children, leaning their tired heads against me as I worked, others looked grimly scandalized, and several of the roughest colored like bashful girls," Lu remembered.

One of her first patients was First Sergeant Robert Bain. Born in Scotland, nineteen-year-old Robert was living in Detroit and working as a salesman when he joined the Twenty-Fourth Michigan Infantry four months earlier. When General McClellan observed their relentlessness in combat, he exclaimed, "They must be made of iron!" earning them their nickname, the "Iron Brigade." The Iron Brigade also stood out for their choice of hat. Instead of wearing the usual kepi, a cap with a flat top and small brim, they wore a flat-top cowboy hat, known as a Hardee, and decorated it with a single ostrich feather. Their distinctive headgear combined with their iron-willed fighting provoked the Confederate soldiers to nickname them "Those damn Black Hats!"

Fredericksburg was Robert's first battle, and it was going to be his last. His arm had been shot off, but he was luckier than some of his comrades. In his regiment alone, four soldiers' heads were blown off. One was his captain's eighteen-year-old son. Grief flooded everyone's hearts when the captain desperately searched the battlefield for his son's head so that it could be buried with his body. While Lu washed Robert, she noticed the peach fuzz mustache on his upper lip quivered, but he tried to smile bravely. "The little Sergeant was merry as if his afflictions were not worth lamenting over," Lu wrote. But he wasn't happy when his curly brown hair was shorn, and he would not let anyone shave his peach fuzz, which he proudly called his beard. Robert was given a clean shirt, underwear, and socks, each marked "U.S. Hosp. Dept."

Lu looked at him with concern as he lay on his bed with his maimed right arm. "Now don't you fret yourself about me, miss," Robert said to her. "I'm first rate here, for it's nuts to lie still on this bed, after knocking about in those confounded ambulances that shake what there is left of a fellow to jelly. I never was in one of these places before, and think this cleaning up a jolly thing for us, though I'm afraid it isn't for you ladies."

Not long after her interaction with Robert, Lu learned there was a captured Confederate soldier among the wounded. He'd been shot in the foot, and his leg would have to be amputated. "Being a red-hot Abolitionist," Lu wrote, "[I] stared fixedly at the tall rebel, who was a copperhead, in every sense of the word [this was also a term for someone in the North who sympathizes with the South], and privately resolved to put soap in his eyes, rub his nose the wrong way, and excoriate his cuticle generally, if I had the washing of him." Although she didn't like him either, Hannah treated him just as well as all the other patients. When Lu approached him, she followed Hannah's lead and pushed her feelings aside. "Shall I try to make you more comfortable, sir?" she asked politely.

"No, I'll do it myself," he replied gruffly.

So much for Southern chivalry, Lu thought. She dropped the washtub at his feet, leaving him to it. She resolved to ignore his existence from then on.

At 12:30 P.M., she helped deliver lunch to the men. A pint and a half of soup was served with meat, two slices of bread, and coffee with sugar and milk. Special attention was given to making sure the coffee was served hot, so it tasted better and kept their spirits up. When Lu noticed that one man hadn't touched his meal, she offered to feed him.

"Thank you, ma'am," he said to her. "I don't think I'll ever eat again, for I'm shot in the stomach. But I'd like a drink of water."

Lu rushed to get him a glass of water, but the water pails had been taken to get refilled. As soon as they were returned, she immediately filled a mug and hurried over to his bed. She noticed that her patient had gone still during the wait. His face was pallid. She leaned down to listen for his breath and touched his forehead. It was cold. She realized he was dead. "I laid a sheet over the quiet sleeper, whom no noise could now disturb," she recorded. "And half an hour later, the bed was empty. It seemed a poor requital for all he had sacrificed and suffered,—that hospital bed, lonely even in a crowd; for there was no familiar face for him to look his last upon; no friendly voice to say, Good bye; no hand to lead him gently down into the Valley of the Shadow; and he vanished like a drop in that red sea upon whose shores so many women stand lamenting."

In the afternoon, Lu accompanied a doctor named Fitzpatrick on his rounds, carrying a tray of rolled lint, packed lint, roller bandages, plaster strips, ligatures, a pincushion with threaded needles, surgical instruments, towels, and sponges. Dr. Fitzpatrick was a tall, handsome Englishman who was very polite. Lu noticed that his hands trembled, but it wasn't from fear. She didn't mention the alcohol on his breath; however, she did reveal that the worse the injury, the more he seemed to like it. "He...seemed to regard a dilapidated body very much as I should have regarded a damaged garment...cutting, sawing, patching and piecing with the enthusiasm of an accomplished surgical seamstress; explaining the process, in scientific terms, to the patient," Lu wrote.

The amputations were scheduled for the next day. In the meantime, Dr. Fitzpatrick examined injuries and performed small surgeries while Lu received her first lesson in dressing a wound. She thought that the doctor wasn't very gentle with his patients, regarding them more as scientific specimens. "He had a way of twitching off a bandage, and giving a limb a comprehensive sort of clutch, which, though no doubt entirely scientific, was rather startling than soothing, and highly objectionable as a means of preparing nerves for any fresh trial," Lu observed. "He also expected the patient to assist in small operations, as he considered them, and to restrain all demonstrations [screams] during the process."

On this particular day's rounds, Dr. Fitzpatrick didn't think anesthesia was necessary. (The two options at the time were either chloroform or ether. Ether was less likely to kill the patient, but, unlike chloroform, it was slow acting and smelled so bad that patients often resisted and gagged.) "The poor souls had to bear their pains as best they might.... [S]carcely a cry escaped them, though I longed to groan for them," Lu wrote. Lu watched while Dr. Fitzpatrick poked about the bone fragments and exposed muscle in a patient's gunshot wound. It was typical for doctors to insert their bare fingers into a wound, especially when searching for a bullet, then using either bullet forceps or a bullet scoop to remove it and any other foreign matter. The soldier tried to suppress a cry but was so overwhelmed by the pain that he fainted. This didn't stop Fitzpatrick, who instructed Lu, "Be so good as to hold this till I finish." She followed his orders but had "a strong desire to insinuate a few of his own disagreeable knives and scissors into him, and see how he liked it." They dressed the wound with a piece of lint moistened with water and covered with oiled silk. Later, Fitzpatrick would check for the formation of pus, which he unfortunately took as a sign that the wound was healing. He also needed to check for gangrene and maggots.

The fetid smell combined with opened windows attracted flies that would lay their eggs in the soldiers' wounds, resulting in maggots. This was especially problematic when wounded soldiers were left on the battlefield for days on end in warm weather. One nurse reported that a soldier's arm "was so mortified that the flesh dropped off and as many as a pint of maggots were got out. It is impossible to keep maggots from some wounds for they multiply in less than a minute."

One surgeon noted that the best defense against them was keeping the wound clean, and that a solution of camphor oil was considered an excellent remedy. "It seems . . . the maggot actually does damage in a wound," he reported. "Although not by attacking the living tissues, but only by the annoyance created by the continual sensation of crawling and irritation which it occasions, and of which the patient often complains bitterly."

The medical rounds took up the better part of the afternoon. One additional task for Lu and the nurses was to write to patients' families so they would know where they were hospitalized. Newspapers also printed the names of the hospitals and wounded soldiers, but often space was limited. Family members could also write or visit the Sanitary Commission in Washington, DC, where the list was updated every day.

Lu enjoyed helping the soldiers write these letters. They all gave accounts of the battles they were in and ended with requests for care packages filled with food. "This I like to do for they put in such odd things & express their ideas so comically I have great fun interiorally while as grave as possible exteriorally," Lu explained. She came upon Robert Bain struggling to write a letter with his remaining hand. When he gave it to her to mail, she noticed he was blushing and saw the words "Dearest Jane" at the top of the letter. The thought cheered her up, and she hoped that when he closed his eyes to go to sleep that night, he would dream of his sweetheart.

At five o'clock a bell rang, alerting the nurses and resting patients that supper was ready. Trays were brought out, and the men were served weak tea with milk and sugar and bread with butter. Eating seemed to be their only pleasure. "I presently discovered that it took a very bad wound to incapacitate the defenders of the faith for their consumption of their rations," Lu wryly observed. Hannah always served generous helpings and was even willing to give up her own ration if there wasn't enough. "I find Mrs. Ropes very motherly & kind," Lu revealed.

After supper, Lu and the other nurses assisted the doctors on their rounds. Medicine was given out, faces were washed, bandages were checked, and lullabies were sung. "By eleven, the last labor of love was done; the last 'good night' spoken. . . . Night and nature took our places. Filling that great house of pain with the healing miracles of Sleep, and his diviner brother, Death."

SHORTLY AFTER Lu began working as a nurse, she developed a cough, just like many of the patients. Hannah marked it down as "purely sympathetic." Lu didn't let it interfere with her work. She was up every morning at the crack of dawn working tirelessly for her patients, whom she affectionately called "my boys" and "big babies." "Though often homesick, heartsick, and worn out, I like it, find real pleasure in comforting, tending, and cheering these poor souls who seem to love me, to feel my sympathy though unspoken, and acknowledge my hearty good-will, in spite of the ignorance, awkwardness, and bashfulness which I cannot help showing in so new and trying situation," Lu wrote of these encounters in her journal.

Each morning, one of the first things Lu did after getting dressed was to dash through the ballroom and banquet hall, opening the windows and doors. The reason? "The air is bad enough to breed a pestilence & as no notice is taken of our frequent appeals for better ventilation I must do what I can," Lu explained. Some of the windows were nailed shut, and the lower sashes could only be opened a few inches. The patients' beds were situated directly under the windows, and the frosty morning air made the men shiver. She would try to make her chilled patients more comfortable by stoking the fire, covering them with extra blankets, and making them laugh. Then she would "continue to open doors and windows as if my life depended upon it. Mine does, and doubtless many another, for a more perfect pestilencebox than this house I never saw—cold, damp, dirty, full of vile odors from wounds, kitchens, wash-rooms, and stables."

The sickening smells didn't help Lu's appetite, but, even so, she would head to the dining room for breakfast. Sitting down at the unpolished table was sweet relief for her aching feet, which was a common complaint among nurses, especially at the Union Hotel Hospital. The old ballroom and banquet hall were divided up into little rooms, which kept the nurses running back and forth, tending to their many patients. "It is as much work to take care of 25 here as it is of 100 in one room. It keeps you on your feet all the time," Hannah Stevenson observed while she was the matron at the hospital.

Mealtime was a chance for Lu to rest momentarily, but she found breakfast disappointing. The "inevitable fried beef, salt butter, husky bread & washy coffee" did not tempt her in the least. As she ate, she focused her attention on the eight women and dozen men talking at the table. Among the hired nurses, there were some very well-educated women. Lu liked kind-hearted Hannah Ropes, and she thought pint-sized Julia Kendall was "the most faithful of workers, too much so for her own good," always refusing to rest. But, also among the nurses, Lu found "a few very disagreeable women whom I don't care to know."

Lu was disgusted by "the sanctified nurse who sung hymns & prayed violently while stealing men's watches & money." Another nurse, who was a "much esteemed lady," wore a devout expression on her face, which had earned the chaplain's approval, until it was discovered that she was urging her patients to leave everything to her in their last will and testament. "Everything here strikes me as very odd & shiftless both within & without, people, manners, customs & ways of living, but I like to watch it all & am very glad I came as this is the sort of study I enjoy," Lu revealed, hoping that her study would improve her writing, but not knowing at the time that it was going to bring realism and authenticity to it. Some of it was also going to remind her of home.

When Lu turned her attention to the conversations the men were having at the table, she found them to be "both ludicrous and provoking." Having grown up surrounded by some of the most progressive thinkers of the era, Lu didn't have patience for condescending attitudes. "The conversation is entirely among themselves & each announces his opinion with an air of importance that frequently causes me to choke in my cup or bolt my meals with undignified speed lest a laugh betray to these pompous beings that a 'child's among them takin notes,'" Lu wrote.

At first, if the topic of slavery ever came up, Lu tried to keep her opinions to herself. She had been warned that there were many Southern sympathizers in Georgetown and Washington, DC. Although she held her tongue, her actions spoke louder than any words. She tested her belief that everyone, regardless of race, should be treated as equals, and Lu's behavior shocked some of the hospital workers.

One time when Lu went into the nurses' kitchen to get some gruel for her patients, she noticed a black baby wobbling about, so she scooped the baby up into her arms. A white woman saw and exclaimed, "Gracious!...how can you? I've been here six months, and never so much as touched the little toad with a poker."

"More shame for you, ma'am," Lu said, no longer able to keep quiet. Lu kissed the baby, and, finding her voice, gave the woman an antislavery lecture.

The racial tension and prejudice in the hospital surprised Lu, especially because everyone was working together to help the Union win the war. But she realized not everyone was an abolitionist, and not everyone believed in equal rights.

After Lu kissed the baby and spoke out against slavery, the woman thought Lu was "a dangerous fanatic." But Lu didn't waver from her beliefs, and the opposition only made her want to speak out against it.

"The men would *swear* at the 'darkies,' would put two *g*s in negro, and scoff at the idea of any good coming from such trash," Lu observed. "The nurses were willing to be served by the colored people, but seldom thanked them, never praised, and scarcely recognized them in the street; whereat the blood of two generations of abolitionists waxed hot in my veins, and at the first opportunity, proclaimed itself, and asserted the right of free speech."

Another hot topic infuriating people—not just in the hospital but throughout the world—was the battle at Fredericksburg, which Hannah called a "murder ground." People wanted to know who was to blame for the "soul-sickening slaughter," and, with the Confederacy's independence still a real possibility, whether it was the end of the United States. While the Confederacy was celebrating its victory, the morale among Union soldiers was so low that tens of thousands of men were deserting.

"Burnside nobody blames.... If in the beginning our President had declared freedom for all, and armed all, the rebellion would not have lasted three months," Hannah wrote. "But the North was not ready to respond to such a scheme and here we are! The true question was, whether we would have our sons sacrificed, or the blacks, for whose freedom this war is waged. We decided, as we always have done, pig-headedly—and now the only way out of this trouble remains just where it did before, only to be gained by *immediate, unreserved emancipation....* But I must not *preach* now, for my *use* is *work*."

Although President Lincoln still had a reputation for being honest, he was blamed for the disaster at Fredericksburg, making him very unpopular. Rumors were running rampant. There was talk of Lincoln resigning or being overthrown and replaced by General McClellan. "The popular heart beats low in response to the outcry of the imbeciles in Washington," the *Bedford Gazette* reported.

The widow's wail goes up to heaven for a husband sacrificed in vain.... The homes of the North are desolate and Richmond is not taken, nor is the Union restored. Is it strange that the people have lost confidence in the President? Is it strange that the war has become unpopular? ... But whatever may be the consequence of this last and most dreadful disaster, and while we know that the President is and will be held responsible therefore, we can only mourn the loss of the brave and good men who fell on the bloodstained heights of Fredericksburg. They fell in vain and we can but honor their gallantry and cherish their memory.

President Lincoln was well aware of his unpopularity. "They wish to get rid of me, and I am sometimes half disposed to gratify them," Lincoln said. "We are now on the brink of destruction." Although Lincoln was blamed, General Burnside took full responsibility for the slaughter, and he offered his resignation to the president. Burnside's soldiers had lost all confidence in his leadership abilities, which caused some high-ranking officers to loudly campaign for General McClellan's return, but Lincoln refused to accept it. In Lincoln's address to the Army of the Potomac, he said, "Although you were not successful, the attempt was not an error, nor the failure other than an accident." He praised the troops for their unfailing courage under the enemy's relentless fire and offered his condolences and sympathies to the families of the dead and wounded. He ended by congratulating them "that the number of both [the dead and wounded] is comparatively so small."

But the number of dead and wounded wasn't small no matter how Lincoln tried to spin it. The Union Hotel Hospital was crowded, overflowing with patients, and more were expected to arrive with even more serious injuries. With the hospital "full of amputated limbs" and other life-threatening injuries and illnesses, Lu and the other nurses had to be off and running right after breakfast. "Till noon I trot, trot," Lu wrote, "giving out rations, cutting up food for helpless 'boys,' washing faces, teaching my attendants how beds are made or floors swept, dressing wounds, taking Dr. Fitz Patrick's orders, (privately wishing all the time that he would be more gentle with my big babies,) dusting tables, sewing bandages, keeping my tray tidy, rushing up & down after pillows, bed linen, sponges, books & directions, till it seems as if I would joyfully pay down all I possess for fifteen minutes rest."

One of the more burdensome responsibilities for Lu and the other nurses was trying to keep their wards clean by motivating the hospital attendants, who were also convalescing patients. The still-sick soldiers were expected to sweep and scrub floors, lift heavy trays, run up and down the many stairs, and move the sicker soldiers. If the attendants didn't perform their duties, the nurses were expected to take care of things. Nurse Sarah Low wrote, "It is something like keeping house with a large family & always expecting company & having very poor help."

Lu found it difficult to work with the two attendants in her ward. "If we had capable attendants things would go nicely," she reasoned, "but sick soldiers being mortal will give out, get cross or keep out of sight in a surprisingly successful manner which induces the distracted nurse to wish she were a family connection of Job's. I have old McGee...& a jolly old soul he is but not a Mercury. My other helper is a vile boy who gobbles up my stores, hustles 'my boys,' steals my money & causes my angry passions to rise." Yet, rather than complain, she moved through her ward like a "ghost from six in the morning till nine at night haunting & haunted for when not doing something I am endeavoring to decide what comes next being sure some body is in need of my maternal fussing."

The reason Lu was so intent was that she wanted to be sent next to a field hospital near the front lines, and she was trying to learn as much as she could about nursing. This meant not shying away from the operations, including amputations, because the surgeon on the battlefield was considered an "amputation specialist." "I witnessed several operations," Lu wrote. "For the height of my ambition was to go to the front after a battle, and feeling that the sooner I inured myself to trying sights, the more useful I should be."

Like the other nurses, Lu would learn that serious head, chest, and abdomen wounds were typically fatal. Operations for these types of injuries were usually out of the question. Surgeons would try to stop bleeding arteries and remove any visible, easy-to-reach bone fragments and bullets. Morphine would help kill the pain, but there wasn't much more that could be done, other than pray. Bullets in or through the feet, legs, hands, and arms, however, were a different story. In these cases, doctors could amputate, and sometimes the patients would survive. But without germ theory and antiseptics, infection and gangrene inevitably followed. "The amputation cases are dying in all hospitals of just poison," nurse Sarah Low observed. "Some think it is an epidemic." Half of the amputees would die. This was better odds than having a chest or abdomen wound, but it was still seven times safer to fight a three-day battle than to have a limb cut off.

One eyewitness chronicled the scene at a field hospital after the First Battle of Bull Run with this graphic description:

Tables about breast high had been erected upon which the screaming victims were having legs and arms cut off. The

surgeons and their assistants, stripped to the waist and bespat-
tered with blood, stood around, some holding the poor fellows
while others, armed with long, bloody knives and saws, cut and
sawed away with frightful rapidity, throwing the mangled limbs
on a pile nearby as soon as removed....Many were stretched
on the ground, awaiting their turn...while those whom operations had already been performed calmly fanned the flies from
their wounds. But...some moved not—for them the surgeons'
skill had not availed.

After the battle at Antietam, the surgeons in the field were
harshly criticized for being too eager to amputate. On Christmas Day in 1862, the *New York Times* reported, "The butchery
practiced by some of the volunteer surgeons on the battle-field
at Antietam will not be repeated again, if it lies in the power of
Gen[eral] Hammond to prevent it....Thigh-bone amputations,
(which some medical butchers take especial delight in practic-
ing, and which all surgical experiments have demonstrated to
be impossible, if saving the life of the patient is the object to be
attained,)...are positively forbidden."

Lu noticed that, in addition to his general roughness with
patients, Dr. Fitzpatrick seemed to enjoy performing intricate
amputations on them. "I find him in a state of bliss over a com-
plicated amputation....[He] works away, with his head upside
down, as he ties an artery, saws a bone, or does a little needle
work with a visible relish and very sanguinary pair of hands," Lu
wrote.

If a patient died, he was taken to the "dead house" located in the basement. Sometimes the doctors would dissect
the bodies. The youngest doctor at the Union Hotel Hospital,

twenty-six-year-old John Winslow, invited Lu to watch a dissection, but she refused. "My nerves belonged to the living, not the dead.... [The] idea was a rather trying one, when I knew the subject was some person whom I had nursed and cared for," Lu wrote. Despite the off-putting invitation to watch a dissection, Lu thought Dr. Winslow, or "Dr. John" as she called him, was a gentleman. But she also thought he was "plain, odd, sentimental...kind-hearted as a woman & rather quaint, being bred a Quaker."

Dr. John had been raised by his aunt and uncle in Massachusetts after his parents died. They loved him as their own son and prepared him for Harvard University by sending him to the prestigious Phillips Exeter Academy. After graduating from Harvard, Dr. John was a teacher for two years before enrolling at Harvard Medical School. But he dropped out. When he learned that the Union army was in desperate need of doctors to treat the massive number of wounded, he offered his services. At the time, a medical degree wasn't necessary to practice medicine, which was considered more of a healing art than a medical science. So anyone could call himself a doctor. But the Union army tried to weed out those with questionable credentials by having them take the required surgeon's and assistant surgeon's exams.

Like most reputable physicians, when Dr. John was trying to figure out how to treat patients, he relied on the best-selling medical book *Treatise on the Practice of Medicine* by the well-known Dr. George Wood. Although the medical treatments weren't based on formal scientific research, they were remedies that doctors had tried on patients. Some of them worked.

For example, if a patient was flushed, had chills, was shivering and sweating, Dr. John would prescribe a dose of quinine to reduce the fever from malaria. Even though malaria was believed to be caused by bad air rather than mosquitoes, quinine works (and is still used today). For a cold, fever, or diarrhea, which was a common and often life-threatening ailment among the soldiers, Dover's Powder, containing ipecac and opium, was prescribed as a possible cure. If a wound became infected, it was believed cutting open a vein and letting the patient bleed would reduce the infection.

Sometimes the doctor would prescribe "blistering" an area of skin on the patient with an irritant, such as powdered Spanish fly. The pus that was formed in the blister was believed to carry away the infection. Spanish fly was also taken internally to treat paralysis, tetanus, and diabetes. For many doctors, like Dr. Stipp, the head surgeon in charge who took Clark's place at the Union Hotel Hospital, the poisonous mercury-based calomel was prescribed if all else failed. There was no agreement among the doctors as to whether calomel was an effective treatment.

When Lu assisted Dr. John on his rounds, she noticed that he treated his patients very differently than Dr. Fitzpatrick did. "Dr. John...goes purring about among the men very friendly, painstakingly & fearfully slow," Lu wrote. He also seemed to feel every patient's pain, often asking, "Do I hurt you?" Most of the patients would say no even if they were clearly in pain. Lu knew this and so, whenever she assisted Dr. John, she would try to take the patient's mind off the pain with witty conversation, so that soon "all three laughed and talked, as if anywhere but in a hospital ward."

When Lu was off duty, Dr. John would stop by her room to drop off books for her. He also invited her back to his room, but she refused. Lu wasn't always a rule follower, and she liked to push the oppressive boundaries placed on women, but she clearly subscribed to the belief that it was not proper for a woman to visit a man's bedroom alone. She did, however, go with him to the capital one night to hear a sermon. Afterward, they went to dinner. She had found the sermon dull and the dinner even duller. "Quotes Browning copiously," Lu described the doctor in her journal. "Is given to confidences in the twilight, and altogether is amiably amusing, and exceedingly *young*."

Lu wasn't interested in a hospital romance (and Dragon Dix wouldn't approve). So the budding romance fizzled, and, soon after their date, Lu was assigned to the night shift, for which she was grateful. "I like it, as it leaves me time for a morning run, which is what I need to keep well; for bad air, food, and water, work and watching are getting to be too much for me," she detailed in her journal. "I trot up & down the streets in all directions, some times to the Heights, then half way to Washington, again to the hill over which the long trains of army wagons are constantly vanishing & ambulances appearing. That way the fighting lies, & I long to follow."

Her new assignment put her in charge of three rooms, which she dubbed "my duty room," "my pleasure room," and "my pathetic room" and sorted her patients accordingly. "One, I visited armed with a dressing tray, full of rollers, plasters, and pins; another, with books, flowers, games, and gossip; a third, with teapots, lullabies, consolation, and, sometimes, a shroud," she wrote.

One of Lu's favorite patients in the "pleasure room" was her "Little Sergeant," Robert Bain. He was one of the luckier amputees, having beaten the odds of further infection, and Lu enjoyed his companionship and good nature. "Many a jovial chat have I enjoyed with the merry-hearted lad, who had a fancy for fun,

when his poor arm was dressed," she recalled of their time together. Even when Dr. Fitzpatrick poked and prodded Robert's
amputated arm, he told Lu that he'd rather laugh than cry. Lu
would read to him from her cherished copy of Charles Dickens's
first novel, *The Pickwick Papers*, to help him brave the pain. "So
just say that bit from Dickens again, please, and I'll stand it like
a man," he said to her. Robert also had a penchant for calling his
fellow wounded soldiers by their afflictions rather than by their
names. There was "Rheumatiz," "Typus," "No Toes," and "Ribs."
At first, Lu was taken aback by his "bandy remarks," but his comrades appreciated his humor, and so did Lu. So, she called him
by his nickname, "Baby B., because he tended his arm on a little
pillow, and called it his infant," Lu explained.

One night Lu went into the "pathetic room" and noticed a
new patient there who was so tall his bed had to be lengthened.
She learned his name was John Suhre. His reputation had preceded him.

One of his fellow soldiers had told Lu he was very worried
about John, who had volunteered to stay behind at Fredericksburg. Even though he was also wounded, John had set his own
needs aside to help his fellow wounded soldiers. His friend was
deeply touched by John's "courage, sobriety, self-denial, and
unfailing kindliness of heart." When John finally arrived at the
hospital a few days after his comrade, Lu watched John from
a distance for two nights before she approached him. "To tell
the truth, I was a little afraid of the stately looking man...who
seldom spoke, uttered no complaint, asked no sympathy, but
tranquilly observed what went on about him," she wrote. When
Lu finally found the courage to speak to him, she would un-
knowingly see her own reflection—a soldier with the qualities

she admired and possessed herself. She would also discover the hero in her stories.

It DIDN'T feel like Christmastime. The weather outside was mild, and the ice on the Potomac River had melted. There wasn't a snowflake in sight.

Inside the dingy and foul-smelling hospital, Lu didn't feel in a particularly festive mood either. Although there were brief moments of cheerfulness and she was settling into her responsibilities, she was still adjusting to her new life as an "embryo nurse" at the hospital. "I [have] never [been]...in a stranger place than this, five hundred miles from home, alone among strangers, doing painful duties all day long, & leading a life of constant excitement in this greathouse surrounded by 3 or 4 hundred men in all stages of suffering, disease & death," Lu detailed in her journal.

News from home was a lifeline, and Lu looked forward to receiving letters from her family and friends. One such letter arrived with the exciting news that her "blood and thunder" story, "Pauline's Passion," won a short-story contest. Although she hadn't received the one-hundred-dollar prize yet, she would once it was published in *Frank Leslie's Illustrated Newspaper*.

Even though Lu didn't have much time to think about it or to write, she grabbed any opportunity she could to reply to her family's letters: "[The] topsey turvey letters [were] written on inverted tin kettles, in my pantry, while waiting for gruel to warm or poultices to cool, for boys to wake, and be tormented, on stairs, in window seats & other sequestered spots favorable to literary inspiration." Lu's mother would read the letters out loud, sometimes with her voice trembling and other times laughing or crying, while Julian Hawthorne and their other neighbors crowded around to listen.

One night Lu was sitting at the bedside of a young soldier whose leg had been amputated when literary inspiration struck. While she patiently watched over him, a rhyme "jingled into [her] sleepy brain": "We sighing said, 'Our Pan is dead.'"

Lu was thinking about the death of Henry David Thoreau, her friend who had taught her botany as a child on nature walks around Walden Pond. She wrote down some lines that expressed her grief and belief that although Thoreau was dead, his spirit lived on. She called the poem "Thoreau's Flute." Later, she put it among her papers. She didn't have time to finish it but thought she would put it in her scrapbook when she returned home.

Lu wasn't planning on going home anytime soon. She was needed at the hospital. So she wouldn't be able to join her mother, father, and sister May at the Hawthorne's home for Christmas tea. Lu would also miss seeing Sophia Hawthorne's glittering Christmas tree, which was topped with an angel that held a shiny gold globe and a scroll that read, "Peace on Earth, Good Will to Men."

But all was not dismal. Hannah Ropes, who had strived to make Thanksgiving special for the sick and wounded soldiers, planned on doing the same for Christmas. At Thanksgiving, which many considered *the* holiday of the year, she hadn't been sure how she was going to manage it. "What is to be done? The good Doctor says we must make the men happy on that day! As though that were possible with a ration of bread and meat! No turkeys and no pies!" she exclaimed in disbelief.

Fortunately, Hannah was friends with Mary Boyce, who was the maternal head of *"the family* of Georgetown." A strong supporter of the Union, Mary told Hannah not to worry. She would make sure there were enough apple, mince, peach, and pumpkin pies for the two hundred and fifty wounded patients.

For Christmas dinner, however, Hannah wouldn't have to ask her friend for help. Mary Todd Lincoln and Elizabeth Smith, the wife of the secretary of the interior, had raised $10,000 to provide Christmas dinner for all the wounded soldiers in the twenty hospitals. President Lincoln himself had donated "a handsome sum" of $650 out of his own pocket.

Mary Lincoln, who had quietly started daily visits to the hospitals not long after the death of her beloved son, wasn't going to receive much recognition for her efforts. The public still hadn't forgotten her shopping spree and decorating expenses. Instead, credit and praise were showered on the "energetic" and "kindly" Elizabeth Smith.

"Large quantities of provisions have been received from the Northern cities to the Christmas dinner, to be given under the auspices of Mrs. Caleb B. Smith to the soldiers in hospitals in this vicinity. Heavy invoices of turkeys, chickens, apples, cranberries, oranges and such other good things as will be required, have been received," the *Alexandria Gazette* reported, without mentioning Mrs. Lincoln's part in it.

Since Hannah didn't have to worry about a shortage of food for the Christmas dinner, she, along with Lu and the staff, tried to make the hospital more cheery and festive. They hung evergreen wreaths and laced garlands throughout the crooked and drafty hallways, in the dining room, and over the doorways and beds. "We trimmed up the rooms & tried to make it pleasant for the poor fellows & they seemed to enjoy it after a fashion," Lu noted.

While helping with the Christmas preparations, Lu was now overseeing forty patients, one of whom was John Suhre, who had at first frightened her. But, after watching him for a night or two, Lu finally found the courage to speak to him, and they became instant friends. "Though what we call a common man, in education & condition, to me is all that I could expect or ask from the first gentleman in the land," Lu wrote in her journal. "Under his plain speech & unpolished manner I seem to see a noble character, a heart as warm & tender as a woman's, a nature fresh & frank as any child's...tall & handsome....Mrs. Ropes and myself love him."

Because of his injury, John was propped up on a stack of pillows in his extra-long bed. There were a dozen other patients in the "stony sort of room, close into the street, without one pleasant, attractive quality." A man with an amputated arm was in the bed next to him, and a man with a "fearful wound through the thigh" was on the other side. John quietly and serenely observed everything that was happening around him. "Thoughtful and often beautifully mild while watching the afflictions of others, as if entirely forgetful of his own...[h]e seemed to cling to life, as if it were rich in duties and delights, and he had learned the secret of content," Lu wrote. She would come to refer to him as the "prince of patients."

There was only one instance that Lu saw a dark shadow cloud his placid expression. While two doctors were examining his wounds, Lu noticed he was anxiously trying to read the expressions on their faces. "Do you think I shall pull through, sir?" he asked one of the doctors.

"I hope so, my man."

When the doctors walked away, his look of consternation was quickly replaced with serenity.

John was one of Lu's easier patients and never once complained. On her way to help a more demanding patient, she might give him a quick nod or stop briefly by his bedside. When she hurried off, she noticed a wistful look on his face as he watched her leave. One night, she asked Dr. Fitzpatrick which patient was suffering the most. The doctor glanced over at John Suhre. "Every breath he draws is like a stab," Dr. Fitzpatrick said. "For the ball pierced the left lung, broke a rib, and did no end of damage here and there; so the poor lad can find neither forgetfulness nor ease, because he must lie on his wounded back or suffocate."

Lu was shocked. "You don't mean he must die?"

"Bless you, there's not the slightest hope for him," Dr. Fitzpatrick answered. "And you'd better tell him so before long; women have a way of doing such things comfortably, so I leave it to you."

Lu wanted to sit down and cry. "It was an easy thing for Dr. P. [Fitzpatrick] to say: 'Tell him he must die,' but a cruelly hard thing to do, and by no means as 'comfortable' as he politely suggested. I had not the heart to do it then, and privately indulged the hope that some change for the better might take place."

Lu looked over at John and saw him sitting up without the aid of an attendant or nurse for support while the doctor dressed the wounds on his back. Because they were so severe, she thought it better for someone with more experience and physical strength to tend to them. John's head was down, and his hands were clasped around his bent knees. At first, Lu thought he was fine, until she saw his tears fall onto the floor. "I had seen many suffer," Lu wrote. "Some swore, some groaned, most endured silently, but none wept. Yet it did not seem weak, only very touching."

Lu felt her heart open wide, and, brimming with empathy, she reached for him, taking his hand. "Let me help you bear it, John."

John smiled with a look of gratitude and surprise on his face. "Thank you, ma'am, this is right good! This is what I wanted!"

"Why didn't you ask for it before?" Lu wondered.

"I didn't like to be a trouble," John replied. "You seemed so busy; and I could manage to get on alone."

At that instant, Lu realized her empathy was her highest good, a gift to help quell his pain and suffering. In that shared moment, she also felt his courage and dignity, which was his gift to her. This exchange would inspire and transform her.

"You shall not want it any more, John," she said.

Lu also understood the meaning behind his wistful look. "Now I knew that to him, as to so many, I was the poor substitute for mother, wife, or sister, and in his eyes no stranger but a friend who hitherto had seemed neglectful; for, in his modesty, he had never guessed the truth [that he would die]," Lu wrote. While the doctor continued to probe, bathe, and dress his wound, John leaned into Lu and squeezed her hand. No one saw his tears but Lu.

WHEN CHRISTMAS finally arrived, Hannah received bad news. There weren't enough turkeys and pies for the Christmas dinner after all. She wasn't sure if it was either a mistake on the list sent in, an oversight, or if someone had stolen the food.

Nevertheless, despite the shortage of food, they made the best of it, cutting smaller slices of pies and portions of turkey, making sure there was enough to go around. "Our Christmas dinner was a funny scramble," Lu reported. The patients didn't express any complaints, at least not to the newspaper reporter from the *Evening Star*, who wrote that the "patients partook of a bounteous repast." The same couldn't be said for the patients at the Armory Square Hospital, which was surprising because it was considered the best hospital in Washington.

According to the reporter, the hospital staff at the Armory Square Hospital had laid out china plates and a big banquet at the usual dinner hour. But, instead of the patients sitting down to eat, the hospital staff enjoyed the feast. The patients had to wait hours for their Christmas dinner, and, when it was finally served, it was given to them on tin plates. "The turkeys and chickens were cut up in a careless manner and the pieces thrown in confusion into a tin dish.... Many of the men complained, and said they would sooner have an ordinary dinner, and have it on time.... The dinner was provided for the *patients*, not for hospital nurses or attendants, and it was the former who should have been first served, and not been obliged to wait...like beggars," read the article on December 26.

The Armory Square Hospital staff strongly denied the story, but the newspaper stood by its report.

Christmas at the Armory Square Hospital wasn't a complete failure though. President Lincoln and his wife, Mary, did make a surprise visit, boosting the wounded and sick soldiers' morale.

"While at the Armory Hospital to-day the President shook hands with nearly all the invalids, and spoke words of kindness and encouragement to each.... His visit was productive of much pleasurable excitement to the wounded soldiers as well as gratification to himself."

All things considered, Hannah remained optimistic about their holiday dinner. "The Christmas celebration was a great success, and the men had plenty of poultry and oysters," she wrote.

It was sometime on Christmas Day that Edward Schrock, the captain of John Suhre's regiment, sat down to write a letter. He had been by the hospital to see John. He would have been there sooner, but he hadn't known at first which hospital John had been sent to. For some unknown reason, John's name wasn't on the list.

This wasn't the first letter he'd had to write to anxious families back home. At the battle at Fredericksburg four of his men were killed and twenty-two injured, including his brother Amos, who was shot in the arm. With pen and paper in hand, he began his letter to John's mother:

> *Your son is at the Union Hotel Hospital in Georgetown....He was in the fight at Fredericksburg where so many brave men lost their lives for their Country's liberty. He fought bravely....He received 2 wounds, the one ball is lodged in his breast. And one passed through his Lungs. I think he cannot live....It would have been very pleasant to have stayed with him during his last hours of suffering on this earth but I can do no more than visit the wounded. He thinks he is getting well but does not know his condition—I gave him some money and left him with a heavy heart expecting never to see the young man again in this world.*

Lu still hadn't found the words to tell John that he was dying. She and Hannah watched over him, anxiously looking for signs that he was getting better. "He is...mortally wounded & dying royally, without reproach, repining, or remorse," Lu wrote in her journal. "Mrs. Ropes & myself...feel indignant that such a man should be so early lost, for though he might never distinguish himself before the world, his influence & example cannot be without effect, for real goodness is never wasted."

During her shift, Lu spent an hour tending to John, trying to make him comfortable. She washed his face, combed his brown hair, and smoothed out his sheets. Sometimes while she was tidying up the table next to his bed, she felt him softly touch her mended gown. "As if to assure himself that I was there," she supposed. "Anything more natural and frank, I never saw, and found this brave John as bashful as brave, yet full of excellencies and fine aspirations, which having no power to express themselves in words, seemed to have bloomed into his character and made him what he was."

It was so difficult and painful for John to breathe that he could only speak in a whisper. He asked Lu to write a letter for him. She sat down in the chair next to his bed with her pen and paper. "Shall it be addressed to wife, or mother?" Lu asked, unable to suppress her curiosity.

"Neither, ma'am; I've got no wife, and will write to mother myself when I get better." He told Lu that his mother was a widow and was still raising his younger sister and brother. He was trying to help keep his family afloat, just like Lu. "We're not rich," John said. "And I must be father to the children and husband to the dear old woman, if I can." John wanted the letter sent to his younger brother, George.

With all his responsibilities to his family, Lu asked him why he had enlisted.

"I wanted the right thing done," John said. "And people kept saying the men who were in earnest ought to fight. I was in earnest, the Lord Knows! But held off as long as I could, not knowing which was my duty; mother saw the case…and said 'Go;' so I went."

"Do you ever regret that you came, when you lie here suffering so much?" Lu asked.

"Never ma'am; I haven't helped a great deal, but I've shown I was willing to give my life, and perhaps I've got to; but I don't blame anybody, and if it was to do over again, I'd do it." He looked at Lu, and as if he was reading her mind, suddenly asked, "This is my first battle; do they think it's going to be my last?"

It was the hardest question Lu ever had to answer. "I'm afraid they do, John."

Her answer seemed to startle him. After a moment, he said, "I'm not afraid, but it's difficult to believe all at once."

"Shall I write to your mother, now?" Lu asked, thinking he might have changed his mind.

"No, ma'am." John still wanted the letter addressed to his younger brother. "He'll break it to her best, and I'll add a line to her myself when you get done." John chose his words carefully, giving advice to his younger brother, "tenderly bequeathing" their mother and sister to him, and bidding him farewell. He wrote a few lines to his mother in his own hand.

Of all the letters Lu had written during her time as a nurse, she thought "John's was the best of all." While Lu sealed the letter, John said, "I hope the answer will come in time for me to see it."

ON THE evening of December 27, Lu was called to John's bed-side. He was dying. "I had been summoned to many death beds in my life," Lu recalled. "But to none that made my heart ache as it did then, since my mother called me to watch the departure of a spirit akin [to Lu's younger sister, Lizzie/Beth] to this in its gentleness and patient strength."

When Lu approached his bedside, John reached out his hands. "I knew you'd come!" he whispered.

Lu sat down in the chair next to his bed while Hannah took the chair on the other side of him. Lu wiped the drops of sweat from his forehead and began waving a fan over him, trying to make him comfortable even though there was little she could do. "I saw the grey veil falling that no human hand can lift," Lu wrote.

In the bed next to John, the patient with the amputated arm was looking over at him with tenderness. The patient on the other side, who had the fearful thigh wound, watched for a bit but then looked away, turning over in his bed and pulling the covers up over his head.

Dr. Fitzpatrick, John's surgeon, wasn't called to his deathbed. There was nothing he could do, and Hannah didn't trust him. "[The] ward physician is in his cups all day! . . . The most import-ant ward in the hospital and the guiding spirit walking among the amputated limbs like a somnambulist," Hannah revealed.

Lu continued to fan her patient while waiting for him to die. John's lips were white, and with each painful breath his body convulsed, fighting against death. At times, he would rip the cov-ers off in his agony. But Lu noticed his eyes never lost the look of serenity. "The man's soul seemed to sit therein, undaunted by the ills that vexed his flesh," Lu wrote.

Hannah noticed this too: "There was in the man such a calm consciousness of life, such repose on its secure strength. There he lay, his broad chest heaving with obstinate breath, but the face composed in its manly beauty, as though he were taking natural rest in sleep. The dignity of the man, considering the circumstances, was wonderful."

The gaslight lamps were burning brightly in the ward. For two hours, John suffered under their glow with each breath, crying out only once, asking for air. All Hannah could give him was a sip of water.

"Thank you madam, I think I must be marching on," John said. He stretched out his right hand, placing it in Lu's lap and reaching for her hand.

"He never spoke again, but to the end held my hand close, so close that when he was asleep at last, I could not draw it away," Lu recounted. When she finally let go, her hand felt cold and stiff. The marks from John's fingers remained even after her hand warmed up. "I could not but be glad that, through its touch, the presence of human sympathy, perhaps had lightened that hard hour," Lu hoped.

Lu got up out of her chair, leaving Hannah alone with John. As Hannah continued to watch him with "loving sympathy," she reached out, touching his forehead with her hand "as though she would cross palms with the angels commissioned to take her work out of her hands."

After a moment, Hannah began preparing his body for burial. She smoothed back his brown hair and cut a lock to send to his mother. She also straightened his long limbs and was so affected by his "wondrous manly beauty" she sent for Lu. Lu returned to John's bedside feeling "a tender sort of pride in my lost patient."

In her mind, "he looked a most heroic figure, lying there stately and still as the statue of some young knight asleep upon his tomb. The lovely expression which so often beautifies dead faces, soon replaced the marks of pain."

While Lu was standing there with Hannah, the ward master handed Lu a letter. It was from John's mother. Lu leaned down and "kissed this good son for her sake" and placed the letter in John's hand, so he "would not be without some token of the love which makes life beautiful and outlives death." As Lu walked away, she felt "glad to have known so genuine a man, and carrying with me an enduring memory of the brave . . . blacksmith, as he lay serenely waiting for the dawn of that long day which knows no night."

Through John, Lu had met her unfulfilled destiny in love and war. He was the soldier she couldn't be, and he was the man her father wasn't. John was physically imposing in his masculinity and unpolished speech, but at his core lived a tender and empathetic caretaker. Like Lu, he wanted to help his family financially, fight for a cause he believed in, and put others first. John was Lu's hero. A noble man who was willing to sacrifice his own needs and desires to give to others, no matter the cost.

Sharing the raw and emotionally intimate experience of John Suhre's pain had opened Lu's heart and awakened her authentic voice. Those intense emotions would transform her work, giving her insight to create characters and stories that would transcend the page and fill her readers' hearts.

Chapter 8

A BITTER PILL

A few days later, Union Hotel Hospital

A FEW DAYS AFTER JOHN'S DEATH, LU WAS TAKING THE stairs and started to cough uncontrollably until she was forced to sit down. Her head felt like it was spinning, so she leaned against the cool banister. Steam from the washroom below puffed and swirled the stench through the hospital's drafty hallways. Lu tried to catch her breath.

"My dear girl, we shall have you sick in your bed, unless you keep yourself warm and quiet for a few days," Dr. John said upon finding Lu on the stairs. He warned her in a paternal manner, just like the other doctors did, that she would soon be sick with pneumonia if she didn't go off duty.

Lu thought him kind but was displeased that he considered her "a frail young blossom, that needed much cherishing, in-stead of a tough old spinster, who had been knocking about the world for thirty years." However, she couldn't ignore the fact that her head felt like a cannonball and that, when she looked at Dr. John, he appeared unnaturally tall while the walls moved in a wavelike motion. "Taking these things into consideration...I resolved to retire gracefully, if I must," Lu decided.

She wasn't the only nurse who wasn't feeling well. A little less than three weeks after the wounded soldiers arrived from the battle at Fredericksburg, most of the nurses were run-down. "The tax upon us women who work for the love of it is tremendous when we have a new arrival of wounded," Hannah explained in a letter to her son, Neddie. Hannah herself was feeling deathly ill, yet her strong sense of responsibility and work ethic kept her from taking care of herself. After she had prepared John's body for burial, Hannah had stayed up all night helping another patient. Soon after, Dr. Stipp, the head surgeon at the hospital, had ordered her to stay in her room where he would check on her twice a day. "My last patient, who was so crazy, whose hand I held so long till he fell asleep, upset me," she wrote. "It was, the Doctor said, 'the drop too much.'" She wrote to her daughter Alice that she had pneumonia.

The pervading medical theory at the time was that damp, cold air invaded the respiratory tract and caused pneumonia. For mild cases of pneumonia, some medical experts advised keeping warm, drinking hot tea, and taking small doses of the flower lobelia combined with either a vapor or footbath to make the patient sweat. Lobelia was touted as a "nauseant expectorant" with no equal. Some considered it the most effective drug for the treatment of "respiratory affections," including colds, pneumonia, asthma, whooping cough, bronchitis, laryngitis, and a sore throat.

The doctors at the Union Hotel Hospital, who were treating Hannah, ordered her to rest in her room, stay warm, and drink some tea. Although her prognosis was good, Mary Boyce wanted her to leave the hospital and recover at her home. But Hannah refused. "I have had the devoted attention of the whole house," she replied to her friend's offer. "And all the surgeons say even if I can't do anything at all, I *must stay* or the house will go down!"

Hannah may have been an ideal patient who listened to the doctors and took their advice, but Lu did not follow her example. Although Lu agreed to go off duty, she had trouble staying in her room and resting. For the first day or two, Lu walked down the flight of stairs to the dining room for her meals. "No one had time to come up two flights while it was possible for me to come down," Lu wrote. "Far be it for me to add another affliction." But this was futile because she couldn't even eat the bread and butter. So Lu decided to try her own "exercise and sun cure," hoping that if she went outside for some fresh air and activity, it would make her feel better. "Every morning I took a brisk run in one direction or another," Lu wrote. "For the January days were as mild as Spring. A rollicking north wind and occasional snow storm would have been more my taste, for the one would have braced and refreshed [my] tired body and soul, the other have purified the air."

On one of her morning runs, she stopped by the Armory Square Hospital, where she had originally hoped to serve as a nurse. She wanted to see how it compared to the one she worked for. Despite the Christmas dinner scandal, it was evident to Lu at first glance that this hospital truly was one of the best. She was impressed with the "long, clean, warm, and airy wards, built barrack-fashion, with the nurse's room at the end." It was a stark contrast to her ward and room, which were "cold, dirty, inconvenient, up stairs and down stairs, and in everybody's chamber."

The Armory's head surgeon, Dr. Willard Bliss, and the hospital steward, Mr. Abram Nichols, were well-liked and held in high regard. On Christmas Day, they were each given a stylish gold watch. Dr. Bliss was also presented with a cane, topped off with a gold handle, as a "memento of the respect and esteem in which he is held by the soldiers on account of his labors for their welfare."

While Lu breathed in the clean air in the Armory, she watched a white-aproned nurse, with her well-stocked supply of medicine, and the well-trained attendants taking care of the sick and wounded and was further impressed. "Here [at the Armory Square Hospital], order, method, common sense and liberality reigned and ruled, in a style that did one's heart good to see," Lu noted. At the same time, it made her feel bad about her own situation. "At the Hurly-Burly Hotel, disorder, discomfort, bad management, and no visible head, reduced things to a condition which I despair of describing."

Despite not feeling better from her "exercise and sun cure," Lu had been eagerly awaiting New Year's, as this was the day President Lincoln would sign the Emancipation Proclamation. At midnight, when the firecrackers and bells rang out through Georgetown, Lu jumped out of bed and opened her bedroom window. She cheered and waved her handkerchief at the shouting black men in the street below, bringing in the New Year and celebrating through the night. When the sun came up, the streets were flooded with people. Women wore their best bonnets and silk dresses, and men were in coattails as they made their way to the White House. Thousands were gathered there, anxiously waiting for the gates to open, so they could meet President Lincoln.

INSIDE THE White House, Lincoln was holding a reception, the first since his son Willie's death from typhoid nearly a year prior. Soldiers and police stood guard at the entrance and lined the hallway. In a parade of dress uniforms, shiny medals, and gold lace, foreign diplomats, politicians, and military officers were the first to pay their respects to the president.

At noon, the gates were opened, and the public poured in, surging through the densely packed hallway. As the crowd rushed forward, bonnets were lost, coattails were torn, and pockets were picked. The people were corralled into Mary Lincoln's recently renovated Blue Room. The oval-shaped drawing room, with its blue frescoed ceiling, overlooked the back lawn and had a view of the Potomac River. The walls were draped with blue and gold hangings, and the floor was covered in blue and white velvet carpet. Mary had chosen wooden chairs and sofas with gold leaf trim and covered with blue and silver satin damask. An aide to Prince Napoleon described the room as magnificent—but "the furniture, though extremely rich, was in rather poor taste."

With the reception in full swing, President Lincoln stood in the middle of the Blue Room with Mary, still in deep mourning wearing a black velvet dress with diamond-shaped trim. Lincoln's familiar stovepipe hat was adorned with a black ribbon in memory of Willie. Lincoln's hair was graying, his shoulders were stooped, his skin was sallow, and there was a "sunken, deathly look about the large, cavernous eyes." Grief had noticeably altered his appearance.

Mary too was still consumed with grief over her son's death. The night before, Mary had met with a spiritualist who claimed to speak to her dead son. One of Mary's friends detailed in his diary, "Mrs. Lincoln told me...she [the spiritualist] had made wonderful revelations to her about her little son Willie who died last winter, and also about things on the earth. Among other things she revealed that the cabinet were all the enemies of the president, working for themselves, and that they would have to be dismissed, and others called to his aid before he had success."

In the face of so much death, grief and uncertainty fueled the fad of talking to the dead. Mary Lincoln would cultivate friendships with various spiritualists, but sometimes she claimed not to need a spiritualist to help her communicate with Willie. "He lives," Mary told her half sister, her eyes wide and shining. "He comes to me every night and stands at the foot of my bed with the same sweet, adorable smile he always had. . . . You cannot dream of the comfort this gives me."

Unlike Mary, Lincoln didn't believe in this practice and was concerned that these so-called spiritualists might be doing more harm than good for his wife's fragile mental state.

Despite Mary's early departure from the New Year's Day reception, Lincoln stayed, shaking hands for hours with a steady stream of people. He was wearing white gloves, and when he finished shaking the last hand, his glove looked like "it had been dragged through a dust-bin."

Mary's Blue Room wouldn't fare much better. Whenever the public visited the White House, chunks of the carpet, wall hangings, and damask-covered furniture were stolen—sometimes even by the person standing guard.

When the reception was over, Lincoln went upstairs to his office. The Emancipation Proclamation was placed before him. When he dipped his pen into the inkwell, his hand trembled. He dropped his pen and looked up. "I never, in my life, felt more certain that I was doing right, than I do in signing this paper," he said. "But I have been receiving calls, and shaking hands since nine o'clock this morning, till my arm is stiff and numb. Now, this signature is one that will be closely examined, and if they find my hand trembled, they will say 'he had some compunctions.' But, any way, it is going to be done!"

Lincoln picked up his pen again and boldly signed his name, effectively changing the meaning and purpose of the Civil War. It was no longer just about keeping the states united. The war was also about freeing the slaves—exactly what abolitionists like Lu had been fighting for and were willing to die for.

BACK AT the Union Hotel Hospital, nearly all the nurses were sick and off duty. Julia Kendall was ordered to stay in bed. Her knee wouldn't bend, and she could no longer walk.

Lu was diagnosed with pneumonia. From her sickbed, Hannah ordered Lu to stay in her room and put a mustard plaster on her chest. While Lu carefully did so, Hannah wrote an overdue letter to her son. "I have been sick, or you should have heard from me sooner. . . . Miss Alcott and I worked together over four dying men and saved all but one, the finest of the four, but whether [due to] our sympathy for the poor fellows, or we took cold, I know not, but we both have pneumonia and have suffered terribly. She is a splendid young woman."

STUCK IN her dreary room, Lu passed the days writing letters to her worried family, sleeping, reading, and trying to "keep merry," but that was proving to be difficult. Lu still wanted to do whatever she could to help win the war. So, she started patching and repairing the soldiers' cotton clothes. Sometimes, while she was sewing for the patients, Lu sat by the drafty window, looking out and taking notes when something captured her interest.

A continuous stream of army carts, each pulled by six mules, rattled through the muddy street. Sometimes the carts were ambulances full of wounded men, and other times they were filled with the dead inside coffins. Officers rode by on horseback, outfitted in uniforms that were occasionally too tight, making them look like "stuffed fowls" to Lu. She thought the women who wore sweeping hoop skirts and big bonnets weighed down with brightly colored flowers looked like a "perambulating flowerbed." And then there were the rowdy pigs that ran free, knocking passersby into the muddy road.

Beyond her view, near Fredericksburg, General Burnside was preparing to cross the Rappahannock River once again and attack General Lee's army. Almost all of Burnside's subordinates were opposed to his new plan, but Lincoln approved it. Regardless, another battle meant more wounded would arrive at the Union Hotel Hospital.

Eight of the ten nurses were sick and off duty. Now that Lu was no longer a nurse but a patient, she had a deeper understanding of how the soldiers felt at the hospital. "I was learning...what the men suffer and sigh for," Lu wrote. "How acts of kindness touch and win; how much or little we are to those about us; and for the first time really see that in coming there we have taken our lives in our hands, and may have to pay dearly for a brief experience."

Every day, the doctors walked up the creaky stairs to check on Lu. She was still suffering from a headache, cough, fever, achiness, and fatigue. And with every breath and cough, she felt a sharp, stabbing pain in her chest. The doctors carefully checked her pulse and tapped her lungs, and they always looked somber, which was not encouraging to Lu.

Dr. John tried to make her feel better by giving her one of his favorite books by English poet Robert Browning. He also sprinkled her with sweet-smelling cologne and stoked the fire to keep her warm. The one doctor who didn't check on Lu was Dr. Fitzpatrick. He had been demoted and transferred elsewhere for drinking on the job.

After the doctors left, the attendants from her ward would stop by to try to cheer her up with news, notes, and presents from her patients. The two nurses who were still on duty would also come by to rest their tired feet by the fireside, chatting and trying to make her comfortable for the night. They also brought meals to her. "My sister nurses fed me," Lu related appreciatively. "Not only with food for the body, but kind words for the mind; and soon from being half starved, I found myself beteaed and betoasted, petted and served."

With a shortage of nurses, the Union Hotel Hospital made an exception and hired a thirty-one-year-old free black nurse, Matilda Cleaver John. And Hannah Ropes's daughter, Alice, was contacted to come to the hospital to help take care of her mother. Alice was glad to be there but not sure what to think of Dorothea Dix and her rules. "Miss Dix does not allow young people in the hospital unless very ugly," Alice wrote to her brother. "But she lets me stay during the daytime, which is not very complimentary to my good looks." Despite the tender care of Alice, the nurses, and the doctors, as each day passed neither Lu nor Hannah improved.

Lu felt as if she were losing track of time, and people started to look strange to her. She struggled to sleep during the night, which was "one long fight with weariness and pain." It was worse if the fire died out, making her room unbearably cold. One wintery night Lu saw Dr. John kneeling in front of the fire, whittling wood shavings and adding logs that he had chopped himself. "I ought to have risen up and thanked him on the spot. But, knowing that he was one of those who liked to do good by stealth, I only peeped at him as if he were a friendly ghost; till, having made things as cozy as the most motherly of nurses could have done, he crept away, leaving me to feel . . . 'as if angels were a watching of me in my sleep,' though . . . [they] do not usually descend in broadcloth and glasses."

With the worsening of their symptoms, the doctors determined that Lu and Hannah weren't just suffering from pneumonia. The pneumonia was a secondary complication to typhoid fever. Dr. Stipp, the head surgeon Lu trusted most, prescribed them both his favorite "cure-all" medicine—calomel—which was one of the recommended treatments for typhoid. Dr. Stipp hoped that the mercury-based "medicine" would cause Lu and Hannah to vomit, purging any illness from their bodies. But the poisonous blue pills didn't help.

"I feel no better," Lu wrote in her journal. "Dream awfully, & wake unrefreshed, think of home & wonder if I am to die here as Mrs. Ropes the matron is likely to do. Feel too miserable to care much what becomes of me."

With Lu's worsening symptoms, the doctors and nurses urged her to go home while she still had the strength to travel. But she refused. "The idea of giving up so soon was proclaiming a defeat before I was fairly routed," Lu explained. "So to all the 'Don't stays,' I opposed 'I will.'" Despite Lu's unwavering resolve, Hannah decided to take matters into her own hands. She agreed with the doctors that Lu should go home. So, without Lu's knowledge, Hannah gave one more order from her sickbed, determined to help one more patient and possibly save one more life.

A few days later, on January 16, Lu was lying in her bed when she saw a gentleman with snow-white hair walk into her room "like a welcome ghost on my hearth." It was Lu's father, Bronson. Hannah had given the order that a telegram be sent posthaste to the Alcotts, informing them that Lu was deathly ill. Once the news arrived, Bronson cancelled his speaking engagements and caught the first train to Washington. "Was amazed to see Father enter the room that morning.... I was very angry at first, though glad to see him," Lu revealed.

Even though it was difficult, when Bronson saw his daughter lying on her deathbed, he maintained his composure, doing his best to hide his shock. Lu was nearly unrecognizable. The typhoid-pneumonia had ravaged his high-spirited and robust daughter into a weak and hollow-cheeked waif. Ever since her last letter home, he'd been worried about her health, and his worst fear had come true. "Letters come from Louisa, giving lively descriptions of hospital scenes," Bronson recorded in his journal. "She seems active, interested, and, if her strength is adequate to the task, could not better serve herself or the country. But I fear this will end in her breaking down." As soon as Bronson saw his daughter, however, he was ready to take her home and "out of the dangers of that infected place." Deep down, Lu wanted to go home. She knew she *should* go home. But she felt it was a disgrace to leave her post. So Lu refused.

Upon Bronson's arrival, Dorothea Dix stopped by Lu's room. She wanted Lu to leave the hospital and recover at a nearby hotel. But Lu felt too sick to even think about moving from her bed, and although she thought Dragon Dix a "kind soul," she didn't like her. "No one likes her & I don't wonder," Lu wrote in her journal, before crossing it out.

The next day, there was a sudden change in the weather, and the bitter cold was blamed for causing Hannah to take a turn for the worse. She was experiencing a violent pain in her chest, making it even harder for her to breathe and talk. The doctors tried to give her relief with a counterirritant. They blistered the skin on her chest, then cut the blisters open, drained them, and added more of the powdered irritant. They hoped this procedure would pull the infection toward the blistered area and away from her lungs, making it easier for her to breathe. But Hannah didn't feel any better.

For the next few days, Bronson waited anxiously for Lu's condition to show any sign of improvement. While he spent time by her bedside in the hospital, he made a point to take a break and visit Lu's ward, wanting to meet the patients that she had written about in her letters. Bronson was in for another shock. Nothing could have prepared the serene and starry-eyed philosopher for the savage and gruesome sights of the wounded soldiers that his daughter had been taking care of. "Horrid war," Bronson wrote. "And one sees its horrors in hospitals if any where."

Bronson also went to the Senate Chamber one evening to hear a speaker. His timing was good, as President Lincoln was there. But Bronson was too worried about Lu to enjoy himself. "I sit near the President," Bronson recorded in his journal. "He has a strong face, and is more comely than the papers and portraits have shown him. His behavior was good, and I respected his honest bearings. I wished to have had an interview, but am too anxious about Louisa, and without time to seek it, nor has he to give. This is not the moment for seeing any one, nor the Capitol to advantage."

On the following day, Hannah was able to get out of bed and, with assistance, walk over to a large chair where she sat down. The change of position seemed to help relieve some of her pain. She looked tranquil while someone lovingly combed her hair.

Although Lu wasn't feeling any better, Bronson wanted her to make the journey home. But rain was coming down hard, and an even fiercer storm was brewing on the horizon, delaying his plans. The doctors didn't want Lu traveling anyway. They thought she was now too sick and weak to make it home.

But later that evening, Hannah died, and the doctors and Lu both suddenly changed their minds.

GLOOM DESCENDED on the Union Hotel Hospital along with the relentless rain, intensifying the grief and suffering at Hannah Ropes's funeral the next day. Usually, when someone died at the hospital, the body was unceremoniously whisked away to the "dead house." And Reverend Snyder, the hospital chaplain, rarely offered any prayers for the dead.

But Hannah's prominent friend, Senator Charles Sumner, who was well known to the public as an ambitious and cold-hearted politician, was devastated by her death. "Mrs. Ropes was a remarkable character," Senator Sumner declared in a letter to his brother. "Noble & beautiful, & I doubt if she has ever appeared more so than while she has been here in Washington, nursing soldiers." Senator Sumner made all the arrangements for her funeral and to send her remains home. Her wooden coffin was placed in the large hall at the hospital, and the patients whom

Hannah had so compassionately cared for gathered around it along with her grief-stricken daughter, friends, and hospital staff. One notable exception was Lu. She was too sick to attend.

The hospital chaplain, whom Lu suspected was a Southern sympathizer, gave the elegy, highlighting Hannah Ropes's many virtues. Among the mourners at the funeral was Hannah's dear friend Mary Boyce. "Everyone about the place looked up to her with affection & reverence, & her influence over the roughest even, among, 'her boys,' as she loved to call them, was remarkable," Mary described the scene. "Whether the great fatigue & privation of comfort during the last six months of her precious life made her less able to resist such an attack no one would like to decide. I shall always feel that she has given up her life to her country, as freely as anyone who died on the field. 'True soldier of the Lord!'" Mary had been agonizing over whether she should have tried harder to persuade Hannah to come home with her to recover. "I have been unhappy at not having Mrs. Ropes under my own roof. But this feeling has changed since conversing with the kind surgeon who attended her so faithfully. He said there was a peculiar fitness in her dying at her post of duty, surrounded by the associations endeared to her."

This was cold comfort for Alice. Her mother's quick demise had caught her off guard. Alice didn't think her mother was dangerously ill until the day before she died, and, even then, she thought her mother was still strong enough to keep fighting. But, as Alice watched her struggling in pain, she was almost relieved when her mother took her final breath and was released from suffering. Even so, the moment her beloved mother died, the loss was too much to bear, and grief overwhelmed Alice, causing her to fall into a violent paroxysm. The doctors gave her a painkiller to help calm her down, but Alice was inconsolable. After Alice's mother's funeral, Julia Kendall held her tightly in her arms, trying to give comfort while sharing the burden of her grief.

Hannah's son, Ned, was also flooded with grief as well as regret. His mother's last wish had been to see him one more time. Senator Sumner had sent a telegram to Ned's commanding officer of the Second Massachusetts Regiment, telling Ned to hurry to his dying mother's bedside. But it arrived too late.

Alice was worried about her brother, fearing he would think he had nothing to live for now. She composed a letter, trying to give him comfort. "I love you very much but feel that *that* will be but small comfort to you and will poorly fill the void created by our dear mother's passing from our bodily vision. But, darling, she is with us all the time, and can tell us our duty and see how much we love her without the use of words.... Our love for her will take us to her, and her great and now divine love for us will be leading us up."

Alice's words did help soothe his pain, and he replied, "Mother was near me last night. It seemed as if I was a little boy, playing on the floor, and mother was sitting, as if knitting, and looking at me very thoughtfully. It seemed also as if she was needed somewhere else, for she did not stay long. It does seem as if mother was nearer to me now than ever before."

Not long after Hannah's coffin was carried out of the hospital and loaded onto the three o'clock train heading to Boston, Lu was carried out. Her patients rallied around her to say good-bye. But Lu was barely aware of them, and she had just a faint idea that she was going home. Lifeless and bone tired, her eyes were half closed. Lu had slipped into a "typhoid state," one of the advanced stages of typhoid fever, as she spiraled closer and closer to death.

At the train station, Dorothea Dix met Bronson and Lu to see them off. She was carrying a basket filled with bottles of wine, tea, medicine, cologne, a small blanket, a pillow, a fan, and a Bible. Before bidding them farewell, Dix gave it to Bronson, hoping it would provide some comfort to Lu.

At six o'clock, the train whistle blew, the engine roared to life, and the iron horse thundered toward Boston, following in the tracks of Hannah Ropes on the long journey home.

Chapter 9

DUTY'S FAITHFUL DAUGHTER

January 24, 1863, Concord, Massachusetts
Three days later

THE SUNLIGHT WAS DYING ON THE HORIZON WHEN THE five o'clock train from Boston steamed past Walden Pond and screeched to a halt at the Concord depot. Lu's younger sister, May, was waiting on the platform. She and her mother hadn't received any news about Lu in a few days, and this was the third evening in a row that May had waited at the train station to see whether her father and sister would be among the passengers.

Ten days earlier, when her father had come home from town with the telegram telling them that Lu was seriously ill of pneumonia, the family was immediately consumed with worry, and Bronson left for Washington. But, the next day, May and her mother received a letter and telegram from Miss Hannah Stevenson, the former matron of the Union Hotel Hospital, who had helped Lu secure her nursing position. Miss Stevenson assured them that Lu was not as ill as they first thought, so they shouldn't worry.

When Bronson arrived at the hospital, he had also sent a telegram with reassuring news about Lu.

"Father is there & she is recovering," May chronicled in her diary. And the letters they kept receiving from Lu also cheered May up. "She is very cross so it's a good sign," May wrote, after reading the letter Lu sent when Bronson showed up at the hospital to bring her home.

May herself hadn't been feeling well for the past week. She had gone ice skating on Walden Pond with Julian Hawthorne and afterward was very sick. But, today after lunch, she was feeling well enough to go to the Emerson's home to read Lu's latest letter.

She always enjoyed reading Lu's letters to friends. Even Moncure Conway, the coeditor of the *Boston Commonwealth*, an antislavery newspaper, had recently stopped by with his wife to hear May read. Afterward, he asked to have the letters copied so he could publish them. May was going to tell Lu this when she saw her.

As the passengers began exiting the train, May searched for the familiar faces of her father and Lu. At last, she spotted them and noticed that her sister was being carried from the train. She rushed over and saw Lu's deathly white face with her eyes rolling up in the back of her head. May was so shaken that she couldn't hide her look of horror and surprise. "I was greatly shocked to find Louy so pale & weak for I had no idea she was so sick," May detailed in her diary.

The long journey had been punishing, worsening Lu's already fragile condition. Bronson had tried to arrive home earlier, but they had missed the previous day's train to Concord by just a few minutes.

Lu remembered little of the past few days. She was only half conscious when they finally reached Boston. But she did notice that, when she was carried off the train, people were staring at her, as if she were a sideshow spectacle. "Louisa was faint and overcome by the long ride," Bronson wrote.

They spent the night in Boston at a friend's house, where Lu "had a sort of fit," prompting a call for a doctor. Lu finally settled down and got some rest, but she was in the vicelike grip of delirium, an advanced stage of typhoid fever. And Lu was having "a dreadful time of it." By morning, however, she seemed a bit better. "Louisa was communicative, and though much spent, seemed far better than I feared," Bronson revealed.

So Bronson and Lu were able to board the four o'clock train from Boston to Concord, but, as the Alcotts made their way home from the train depot to Orchard House, the pain and uncertainty surrounding Lu's condition made it seem like a funeral procession. Lu was taken upstairs to her bedroom. But, even at home in her own bed with the fireplace blazing, Lu found no relief or comfort. In the throes of delirium, she was plagued with nightmares, convinced that the house was roofless and no one wanted to see her.

Her mother was heartbroken at the sight of her daughter teetering on the brink of death, and Abba, whose heart still ached with grief over Lizzie's death, was overcome with fear that she might lose another beloved daughter. "Poor Louy," her mother wrote. "She left us a brave handsome woman...and is returned to us almost a wreck of body and mind."

Her mother didn't have a moment's rest, refusing to leave Lu's bedside. The next morning, Dr. Bartlett, the teetotaler town doctor, made a house call to check on Lu.

"All of us are very anxious about Lu as she is exceedingly feverish & her throat seems almost entirely filled up," May noted.

The doctor diagnosed her with typhoid and was surprised that Lu wasn't in worse shape after such a grueling journey. He gave the Alcotts a lifeline of some much-needed hope to cling to. "Dr. Bartlett has seen her," Bronson wrote, "and thinks, that with quiet and good nursing she will be up again before long. Her trouble is sore throat, with fever at times. She sleeps more or less, and talks at times in her usual lively way."

But Lu's mother didn't have much faith in doctors or their medicine. "I hate Drs. and all their nonsense," she wrote. Abba also didn't want anyone outside of the family to be Lu's nurse. "The efficacy of good nursing I do know and appreciate. And believe if she is to be saved from violent death or the stern ravages of chronic ailments, it will be by faithful vigilant care."

Lu's parents kept vigil by her bedside, taking turns throughout the day and night. They didn't want May to be near her too often, as they were afraid their youngest daughter would catch Lu's illness. "Neither she nor father like to have me about her much as not being very well myself. They think I am very liable to take it, if I am over her too much," May wrote.

Lu's older sister, Anna, who was living eighteen miles away in East Boston, was seven months pregnant, hoping to have a baby girl she planned to name Louisa. Abba wanted to protect her oldest daughter from the truth about Lu's illness. So, when Bronson wrote to her, he was careful with his choice of words, not wanting to cause her any alarm. "Louisa is here at home again," Bronson wrote to Anna. "Though much enfeebled by her sickness and the long journey. She was hardly able to come away, but came through with courage, and less harm than I anticipated.... It was most fortunate for her that I went to her as I did. Every thing was against her at the Hospital."

As Bronson watched Lu fight to survive the ravages of war, he recognized that what he had previously thought were flaws in Lu were assets. The daughter he called a demon was willing to go to hell and back, while she steered proudly and adventurously toward the heaven of her hopes. The stronger the opposing gale, the more determined she was, willing to sacrifice herself for the greater good. Whether it would cost her life he did not know, but he respected her willingness to put her life on the line, testing her ideals and beliefs.

For the next few days, delirium continued to plague Lu. With hallucinations haunting and twisting her mind, she barely knew what was going on around her. And, many times, she was furious in her delirium. Her mother, dressed in black, tried to comfort her.

"Lie still, my dear," her mother said, touching Lu with her soft hands. But, in Lu's mind, her mother had been transformed into a menacing Spaniard, who was always chasing and frightening her. In a recurring nightmare, he was Lu's husband, and he would suddenly walk out of her closet, come in through the window, and torment her all night long.

Compounding the delirium were the fever fits, a type of seizure triggered by her high temperature. The convulsions sometimes lasted several minutes, causing her bloodshot eyes to look wild with fear. Her cheeks would flush to a mahogany red, while her heart pounded and the pain throughout her body intensified.

"She dreads the fever fits which come twice in twenty-four hours, and leave her perplexed and exhausted," Bronson recorded. "But sleep follows to refresh her wasted spirits and give intervals of comparative ease. We hope the fever has not many days more to run."

In the hopes of curing her delirium, Dr. Bartlett blistered Lu's head by applying a plaster of dried and crushed beetles. He continued to stop by every day to check on her. "The Dr. pronounced her, if no better, not worse," Bronson informed Anna.

After nearly a week, Lu's mother was so run-down that she was forced to leave Lu's bedside to get some rest. But she would be back by Lu's side in less than an hour. "Mother giving out as the watching & constant anxiety is too much for her," May worried. Although Abba wasn't feeling well, she didn't consult the doctor. She was taking care of it herself using homeopathic remedies to help alleviate her ailments. But it was also her resolve to keep her daughter alive that kept Abba on her feet, knowing that if Lu were to die, it would be an "insurmountable calamity" for the family. The Alcotts were waging a "fierce campaign, one of the fiercest of the war."

Occasionally, Lu seemed awake and aware. She told her parents stories about the hospital and seemed to be able to read Hannah Ropes's obituary. She was also very interested in how she got home. "She asked me to sit near her bedside, and tell her the adventures of our fearful journey home. . . . [Lu] enjoyed the story, laughing over the plot and catastrophe, as if it were a tale of her imagining," Bronson wrote. But afterward, Lu didn't remember anything, as her fever spiked and the delirium raged. Lu didn't know where she was and was terrified that she would never get home.

One night, Lu became so frightened of the sinister Spaniard that she got up and made a plea to the pope while trying to speak Latin. "If you will only take that man away, I can bear the rest," Lu pleaded.

She was also reliving disturbing scenes from the hospital. In one, Dr. John Winslow and two other nurses were trying to tempt Lu to worship the devil. In another, Lu was tending to millions of sick and wounded soldiers who never died but also never got better. The nightmare caused Lu such distress that she tried to get out of bed and fell to the floor. Her mother, who had left the room momentarily, was in hysterics while May dragged Lu back to bed.

"How could you leave me alone when the room was full of men!" Lu exclaimed.

Her delusions continued, and, at one point, Lu found herself in heaven and saw people flying. Dorothea Dix was among the people there. But Lu didn't like it, finding it dismal and ordinary, and she wished she wasn't there. Another time, Lu believed she was being hunted down by an angry mob in Baltimore. They were breaking down the door, accusing her of being a witch. Lu was tortured as they tried to kill her by hanging, burning, and stoning.

It wasn't until early February that Lu finally found some relief when her fever abated. Exhausted and weak, she couldn't remember much of anything that had happened in the past three weeks. But she had recovered some of her senses. Lu was feeling famished and noticed her throat and mouth were painfully sore. But that wasn't the worst of it. Lu was shocked to discover that her beautiful long hair was gone.

"WAS TOLD I had had a very bad typhoid fever, had nearly died & was still very sick," Lu wrote. "All of which seemed rather curious for I remembered nothing of it."

But Lu did, in fact, remember her sister's shocked face and her mother's look of bewilderment when she arrived home. And the terrifying nightmares were still vivid, lingering in her mind.

"Never having been sick before it was all new & very interesting when I got quiet enough to understand matters," Lu wrote.

When Lu looked in the mirror, a gaunt face and big eyes stared back at her. She didn't recognize herself. And she was still shocked and upset that Dr. Bartlett had shaved her head to blister her scalp. But Lu tried to make the best of it by wearing a hat along with a frisette, so she would have a little fringe of curls that peeked out along her forehead. Still, she couldn't help but mourn the loss of her striking chestnut-colored hair. "Had all my hair, 1 1/2 yard long, cut off & went into caps like a grandma. Felt badly about losing my one beauty," Lu lamented. Trying to cheer herself up nevertheless, she continued, "Never mind, it might have been my head, and a wig outside is better than a loss of wits inside."

She asked impatiently for food. But it was too painful to chew and swallow because her tongue was swollen, her throat was ulcerated, and her teeth were achy and sensitive. Dr. Stipp, the head surgeon at the Union Hotel Hospital, had poisoned her by prescribing too much calomel, and Lu was suffering from the toxic effects of the large doses of the mercury-based blue pills. So, for now, she was given beef tea to drink.

"We trust the main perils are past, and that her recovery dates from this hour, though it will need careful nursing for some weeks to restore her strength and right-mindedness," Bronson wrote.

Lu's entire body was in pain, and she was too weak to walk. Lu was devastated, and she burst into tears. Lu didn't know herself anymore. Always the caretaker, she was used to being independent and physically active, reveling in her morning runs and long walks. But now if she wanted to sit up, Lu had to be carried to the easy chair. "Active exercise was my delight," Lu explained. "From the time when a child of six I drove my hoop round the Common without stopping, to the days when I did my twenty miles in five hours and went to a party in the evening."

Even though her family still sat vigil by her bedside, Lu's pain and suffering seemed to make time slow down. "Such long, long nights—such feeble, idle days, dozing, fretting about nothing, longing to eat & no mouth to do it," Lu recalled. Relentless feelings of gloom and discouragement overwhelmed Lu. "Tried to sew; read & write & found I had to begin all over again." She didn't believe she was getting better, convinced that Dr. Bartlett "had not detected the secrets of her malady." Lu's suffering was so great that she wanted to die.

When Lu's older sister, Anna, was finally told the distressing truth about Lu's condition, she hurried home to Orchard House. As soon as Anna saw Lu, her first thought was of Lizzie (Beth). Lu looked just like her right before she died.

Abba Alcott was so upset about her daughter that she confided in her neighbor, Sophia Hawthorne. Sophia was no stranger to life-threatening illnesses. A few years prior, her oldest daughter, Una, had suffered from malaria for several months, and after recuperating, she then contracted typhus. Although she ultimately recovered, she never fully regained her good health.

Sophia's own health was delicate. As a devoted mother and wife, she had dedicated herself to her daughter's recovery at the expense of her own well-being. And it was only recently that her husband, Nathaniel, who had not been feeling well for months, seemed to be "decidedly better."

Since Lu's arrival home, Sophia had done whatever she could to help and had insisted on making meals for May every day. So, as Abba poured out her heart to her friend, expressing her worst fears about Lu, Sophia listened compassionately.

On February 18, a woman named Mrs. E. A. Bliss showed up at Orchard House. She worked as a maid and companion for the wife of the outspoken abolitionist Horace Greeley. But this was just Bliss's day job. On the side, she used her "magnetic power" to discover people's ailments. It isn't clear who contacted the spiritualist.

Bliss was taken upstairs to Lu's bedroom. She didn't ask Lu any questions. Instead she reached out and held her hands. Closing her eyes, Bliss started "reading" Lu. She told Lu that she had discovered the "internal maladies" plaguing her. No names of the maladies were given.

Shortly after Bliss left, Lu sat up, swept her legs over the side of her bed, and stood up by herself. Then she walked across the room, without any help. She was able to stand for a few moments, so her sister, Anna, could do a fitting for the flannel dressing gown that she was sewing for her.

The next day, the excruciating pain in Lu's back, arms, and legs was gone. Lu climbed out of bed and walked downstairs all by herself. She stayed for an hour.

On Sunday, February 22, it was a bitterly cold morning when Lu woke up. The fireplaces were burning brightly. Downstairs in the kitchen, a hired servant, whose service was a gift from the Emersons, was cooking breakfast.

"Louy down stairs & dressed for the first time," May recorded in her diary. "She is very feeble but entirely herself. She has on her new flannel dressing gown & it is very pleasant to see her about again."

A month later, Lu was still a "rack a bones," but she was eating more regularly and had some more flesh on her body. She could sit up for most of the day and walk a little more around the house. "Falling back in my old ways," Lu wrote. "My first job was characteristic, I cleaned out my piece bags & dusted my books, feeling as tired as if I'd cleaned the whole house."

Among her belongings, Lu found "Thoreau's Flute," the few lines of poetry that she had written one night while watching a soldier die at the hospital. She had forgotten about it. Although she didn't think poetry was her forte, Lu decided she would finish writing it. She still wanted it for her scrapbook.

With Lu's improved condition, the anxiety surrounding her recovery faded a bit, and the family focused their attention on Anna and her coming baby. Bronson went to Boston to hold some philosophical conversations and to be near her while everyone waited eagerly for the arrival of good news.

On Saturday, March 28, snow was falling steadily, and Lu, May, and their mother had given up hope that Bronson would be back from Boston that night. So they made themselves cozy in the parlor and were deeply involved in a novel they were reading out loud when Bronson suddenly burst through the front door. "Good news!" he said, waving his bag in the air. "Anna has a fine boy."

There were peals of laughter and tears of joy. "With one accord, we three opened our mouths & screamed for about two minutes," Lu wrote to her sister Anna. "Then mother began to cry, I to laugh, & May to pour out questions, while Papa beamed upon us all shiny, red & damp yet the image of a proud, old Grandpa."

May wasn't as enthusiastic as Lu, writing in her diary, "Father brought the good news that Annie had a little son. . . . I think we are rather disappointed that it is not a girl."

The following morning, Lu was so anxious for more news about the baby that she "toddled" into town to check the mail. It was the longest distance that she had walked since she had gotten sick, and she didn't feel worn out. The next day, Lu's mother went to Boston to see her first grandchild, and Lu started to do some housework, something she usually despised. "I fell to cleaning house as good work for an invalid & and a vent for a happy *Aunt*," she wrote.

By April, Lu was writing again. Frank Sanborn, the coeditor of the *Boston Commonwealth*, wanted to publish the letters that she had written home while she was working in the hospital. "Sanborn asked me to do what [Moncure] Conway had suggested & teased about . . . to arrange my letters in a printable shape & put them in the *Commonwealth*," Lu noted. "They thought them witty & [sym]pathetic. I didn't, but I wanted money."

Lu's worry about the family's debts weighed heavily on her mind. She had only made ten dollars working as a nurse, and now she had a doctor's bill to pay. But as Lu's strength returned, allowing her to enjoy longer walks in the springtime air, her spirit felt renewed. "Felt as if born again," Lu confided in her journal. "Everything seemed so beautiful & new. I hope I was, & that the Washington experience may do me lasting good. To go very near death teaches one the value of life, & this winter will always be a very memorable one to me."

Despite nearly losing her life and putting her family into more debt, Lu didn't regret her decision to fight for liberty and freedom. "I never shall regret the going," Lu wrote. "Though a sharp tussle with typhoid, ten dollars, and a wig, are all the visible results of the experiment; for one may live and learn much in a month. A good fit of illness proves the value of health; real danger tries one's mettle; and self-sacrifice sweetens one character."

Although Lu didn't have any regrets, her parents did. Realizing too late how dangerous it was for their daughter, her mother and father both lamented encouraging her to go to the front lines. "That was our contribution to the war," Bronson told his mother in a letter. "And one we should not have made willingly had we known the danger and the sacrifices." Lu's idealistic father was shaken to the core by the ruthless reality of what he'd seen at the Union Hotel Hospital and Lu's struggle to stay alive. The raw and unforgiving nature of war pushed him to realize that his daughter's rebellious streak was not a flaw but a strength. Although he had always disapproved of his daughter's motivation to make money, he could not deny what he had witnessed: Lu's courage and willingness to go to the front lines and risk her life for what she believed was right. He could see clearly the huge sacrifice his daughter had made to drive change and make the world a better place. Bronson could finally behold his wayward daughter's innate goodness.

Lu had, at long last, earned her father's approval, and it was the salve to the hurt and pain in their tenuous relationship. Years later, when it was evident that she would never fully regain her good health, her father would be inspired to write a poem for her, the last line of which was "I press thee to my heart, as Duty's faithful child."

Chapter 10

A GIFT

June 1863, Concord, Massachusetts
Two months later

Upstairs at Orchard House, Lu was in her bedroom, wrapped in her green and red glory cloak and mostly recovered with her gold and ivory pen in hand. She was sitting at her half-moon desk sandwiched between two windows. Next to Lu's desk, her sister, May, had recently painted a panel of calla lilies and bright nasturtiums. But Lu didn't need to look out the windows or at art for inspiration. "People mustn't talk about genius—for I drove that idea away years ago.... The inspiration of necessity is all I've had, & it is a safer help than any other," Lu penned.

Now all she had to do was look around her bedroom. It was decorated with new furniture, and, best of all, Lu had not only bought it herself but also for her family. Their bedchambers were now furnished with new bureaus, mirrors, and sleigh beds adorned with colorful handmade quilts. Her mother also received a new worktable for her needlework.

The redecorating wasn't just in their bedrooms. For the downstairs parlor, Lu had purchased new green-patterned carpet as a nice contrast to Bronson's burgundy-colored study across from it. The pretty muslin curtains, which were made from old party dresses, danced lazily over the windows.

May had been busy hanging earth-toned wallpaper, so the paintings, which included some of her own, would stand out. She had also painted murals in some of the rooms, favoring Greek and biblical images.

For years, Lu and her family had talked wistfully about new furnishings for Orchard House, or, as Lu liked to call it, "Apple Slump." So, when she received the one-hundred-dollar prize money from *Frank Leslie's Illustrated Newspaper* for her story "Pauline's Passion and Punishment," Lu paid her family's debts and then splurged on the new furnishings and redecorating.

Lu was feeling hopeful, so she went back to work on her love-triangle novel called *Moods*. She was encouraged by readers' responses to the four "Hospital Sketches" she had written for the *Boston Commonwealth*. They were showering her with praise.

David Atwood Wasson, a transcendentalist writer and minister, had written to her, "Let me tell you what extreme pleasure I have taken in reading 'Hospital Sketches.' Written with such extraordinary wit & felicity of style, & showing such power to portray character!" And Lu was thrilled when she received a letter from the father of Wilkie and Henry James. The prominent theologian found her stories of hospital service "charming." He went further to say, "I am so delighted with your beautiful papers, and the evidence they afford of your exquisite humanity, that I have the greatest desire to enroll myself among your friends."

No one was more astonished by the success and popularity of her work than Lu herself. "Much to my surprise they made a great hit, & people bought the papers faster than they could be supplied," Lu recounted.

The public was hungry for stories about the war from the front lines, especially after another morale-crushing Union defeat at Chancellorsville in May 1863. Lu's "Hospital Sketches" were some of the first published stories about the soldiers wounded in battle and their medical care. It was a grim and somber subject, but Lu's natural ability to bring cheerfulness and humor to the most heartbreaking situations made her readers laugh and cry. Lu's firsthand experience of the casualties of war gave a fresh perspective from a female nurse's point of view, and, through her writing, Lu expressed her beliefs about slavery and women's rights. "I find I've done a good thing without knowing it," Lu noted.

When Lu wrote about dying soldier John Suhre, readers and critics were moved to tears, calling it unforgettable. "The contrast between comic incidents and the tragic experience of a single night...is portrayed with singular power and effectiveness. 'The death of John' is a noble and touching feature," the *Boston Transcript* reported. After reading the review, Lu revealed in her journal, "'A Night' was much liked, & I was glad, for my beautiful 'John Suhre' was the hero, & praise belonged to him."

John Suhre had left an indelible mark on Lu's heart and writing. Together, Lu and John had been two soldiers on the front lines, fighting side-by-side to the death for a greater good. He provided a male contrast to Bronson's presence in her life, one that was more similar to her own traits and values. In her writing, her characters would consistently embody the qualities she and

John shared—courage and kindness. In their intimate moments, he taught her the importance of humane and loving relationships, and how they affect a person's well-being. Drawing from her deep well of empathy, Lu could create realistic and relatable characters that sparked lasting emotional responses from her readers.

Lu was also daring to reveal more of herself through her writing. When Lu was working in the hospital and hurriedly wrote letters home to her family on "inverted tin kettles" while waiting for gruel to warm and poultices to cool for her patients, she wasn't thinking about getting the letters published. Her intention was not about money but to communicate honestly with her loved ones. Lu didn't hide behind a pen name; she was showing and expressing her true self. Her hospital stories were unfiltered Lu, and the readers, including her family, responded positively. "One gets acquainted with her more from her stories than by being with her, & finds what her real character is," shared her sister May.

"Hospital Sketches" were so popular that two publishers wanted to make a book of them. She had to choose between Roberts Brothers and James Redpath, a journalist and fierce abolitionist who had been a friend of John Brown. "I preferred Redpath & said yes, so he fell to work with all his might," Lu explained. Mr. Redpath planned to help victims of the war by donating a portion of the book's profits to the children who were left fatherless or homeless. Lu also thought about giving some of her earnings to the war orphans, but she knew it wasn't practical. Feeling ungenerous, Lu explained her circumstances to Mr. Redpath: "I too am sure the 'he who giveth to the poor lendeth to the Lord' & on that principle devote time & earning to the care of my father & mother, for one possesses no gift for money making & the other is now too old to work any longer for those who are happy & able to work for her.... All that is rightly mine I prefer to use for them much as I should like to help the orphans."

To Lu's surprise, "Hospital Sketches" wasn't her only literary success. Without her knowledge, Bronson had shown her poem, "Thoreau's Flute," to neighbor Sophia Hawthorne. Sophia was very knowledgeable about literature and art, and not just because she was the wife to best-selling writer Nathaniel. She herself had once shown great promise as a writer and artist. But she had given it up to devote herself to raising her children and caring for her family. Even though her husband wrote compassionately about the rigid roles society defined for women, he didn't always encourage Sophia to develop her artistic talents.

Nevertheless, Sophia was so moved by the poem that she felt compelled to tell her friend Annie, who was married to James Fields, the editor of the *Atlantic*, even though Fields had unceremoniously dismissed Lu's talent and ambition, telling her to stick to her teaching. In a letter to Annie, Sophia wrote, "Upon quietly reading it to myself, I find it really emotionally beautiful in form, expression and thought.... It is altogether in a superior tone to any thing I have ever seen of her—so sweet, majestic and calm and serious."

Sophia found Lu's poem so inspiring, she drew a pen-and-ink sketch related to it. Sophia also asked Annie to read it out loud to her husband. As a result, James Fields decided he wanted to publish it.

"Of course I didn't say No," Lu wrote. "It was printed, copied, praised & glorified—also *paid for,* & being a mercenary creature I liked the $10 nearly as well as the honor of being a 'new star'

& 'a literary celebrity.'" Lu had the additional satisfaction of Mr. Fields eating his words once more. As it so happened, he liked not only her poem but also her "Hospital Sketches" and wanted her to write an original war story for the *Atlantic*. Lu didn't say no to that either and wrote "My Contraband," an antislavery story set in a hospital.

In August, Lu's younger sister, May, left home and traveled to Clark's Island in Plymouth Bay. May had been feeling very lonely. Many of her friends were away on vacation. Her near-constant companion, Julian Hawthorne, had been spending more time in Cambridge, preparing to enter Harvard. And his sister, Una, and May weren't getting along. May wasn't sure why, but she'd been excluded from Una's birthday celebration.

May felt very conflicted and unhappy. She was struggling with feelings of envy and guilt for feeling envious.

"I have every blessing," May confessed. "Yet I am a discontent, selfish, ambitious girl, envious of my neighbors' wealth and position, not realizing we are better off ourselves than we ever have been before. I seem to have lost all my good spirits & don't know what to think of myself."

May had also turned twenty-two years old, and although she had ambition to become an artist, she was aware that spinsterhood was fast approaching.

"I am growing very old & feel it too which is silly I know," May wrote the night before her birthday.

Lu offered to treat her sister to a trip, so May could spend time with "pleasant people" and have fun "boating, singing, dancing, croqueting & captivating." May was grateful to her older sister, writing in her diary, "How generous Louisa is to so willingly pay my expenses.... It takes a great deal of pluck to earn money & then hand to another person to spend, but I think her very noble."

Lu spent most of her waking hours at her desk, writing more stories and proofreading her manuscript for Mr. Redpath. Her family was worried she was working too hard, and they feared the worst, with good reason. "I cannot work very steadily without my poor old head beginning to ache & my family to predict relapses," Lu wrote. Despite this, Lu wanted to "be ready in case a discerning public demand further gems from my illustrious pen."

On August 28, Lu's hard work paid off when *Hospital Sketches* was published in book form. "My first morning glory bloomed in my room, a hopeful blue, & at night up came my book in its new dress," Lu noted.

Lu's family shared in her glory. "I see nothing in the way of a good appreciation of Louisa's merits as a woman and a writer. Nothing could be more surprising to her or agreeable to us," her father wrote.

Hospital Sketches also received rave reviews. The New York *Independent* praised it: "The wealth of curious humor, graphic picturings of hospital life, strong good sense, and thorough good-heartedness, took such entire possession of their readers.... Buy it; it is wonderfully enjoyable."

Much to Lu's delight, her book was selling quickly. "I have the satisfaction of seeing my town folk buying, reading, laughing & crying over it wherever I go," Lu recounted. "One rash youth bought eight copies at a blow & my dozen would have gone rapidly if I had not locked them up." Lu gave away three of her personal copies, one of which went to her second-favorite patient, Sergeant Robert Bain (a.k.a. "Baby B.").

Baby B. was now wearing a false right arm, and he was "as jolly as ever" in his letters to Lu. He still wasn't married, despite pouring his heart out to his "Dearest Jane" when he first arrived at the hospital. Instead, he was attending Oberlin College even though he'd rather grab his rifle and go back to his regiment for "another dig at those thundering rebs."

Lu also received a letter from one of the Union Hotel Hospital's surgeons after he read *Hospital Sketches*:

> *To say that I thank you for writing them from the bottom of my heart, would but poorly express the sentiment which dictates to me this minute, & to say that I feel humbled by the lesson which they teach me is to pay a tribute to them which I fancy will be rather unexpected. . . . These papers have revealed to me much that is elevated and pure, and refined in the soldiers' character which I never before suspected. It is humiliating to me to think that I have been so long among them with such mental or moral obtuseness that I never discovered it for myself, and I thank you for showing me with how different eyes and ears you have striven among "the men" from the organs which I used on the very same cases and at the same time.*

Even though Lu was enjoying more success with her writing, she yearned to advance the cause of human rights. She considered traveling to Port Royal in South Carolina, a Union-held territory, where former slaves, or "contrabands," were being educated and trained for jobs. Lu hoped to be a teacher there and to write about her experience in another series of sketches. Based on the success of *Hospital Sketches*, Mr. Fields expressed an interest in publishing them. "I should like of all things to go South

& help the blacks as I am no longer allowed to nurse the whites," Lu penned in a letter. "The former seems the greater work, & would be most interesting to me."

But, because Lu wasn't married, she was turned down by Edward Philbrick, a fellow Bostonian and abolitionist who was a superintendent with the Port Royal Experiment. "Mr. Philbrick objected because I had no natural protector to go with me, so I was obliged to give that up. . . . I was much disappointed as I was willing to rough it anywhere for a time both for the sake of the help it would be to me in many ways, & the hope that I might be of use to others."

So, armed with her gold and ivory pen, Lu supported her causes through her storytelling. By November the trees were shedding their leaves, and Lu was no longer wearing a wig. Her father had harvested the apples from his beloved orchard and stored them in the cellar for winter along with his barrels of hard cider. Lu paid to have the roof shingled and repairs made to the house. "I proudly paid out of my story money," Lu noted, then joked, "I call the old house 'the sinking fund' as it swallows up all I can earn."

Lu was trying to finish two novels, *Moods* and *Success*, a story about her own oppressive experiences as a woman trying to break into the workforce. Mr. Redpath and Mr. Fields were interested in both novels. Lu thought the world must be coming to an end as her dreams started to come true:

> If ever there was an astonished young woman it is myself, for things have gone on so swimmingly of late I don't know who I am. A year ago I had no publisher & went begging with my wares. . . . There is a sudden hoist for a meek & lowly scribbler

who was told to "stick to her teaching," & never had a literary friend to lend a helping hand! Fifteen years of hard grubbing may be coming to something after all & I may yet "pay all the debts, fix the house, send May to Italy & keep the old folks cosy," as I've said I would so long yet so hopelessly.

When she wasn't writing, Lu still found time to attend anti-slavery meetings and help with the Soldiers' Aid. One year earlier, Lu had sent Wilkie James a care package for his "jollification & comfort." This time, she was helping make an afghan for him.

Wilkie had joined Colonel Robert Shaw's Fifty-Fourth Massachusetts Infantry Regiment, the first of two black regiments. Wilkie was an officer and had fought heroically in a deadly and unsuccessful charge on Fort Wagner in South Carolina. He was severely injured with near-fatal wounds in his legs and feet. But he was home now, recovering. "He now lies on a sofa & needs a pretty blanket to cover him," Lu reasoned.

While Wilkie was recovering on the couch, he read *Hospital Sketches*. Like his father, who had written to Lu after reading it, telling her it was "charming," Wilkie also felt compelled to write Lu. "Your wonderful little book was received while suffering much from my wounds. Greatly am I indebted to you for it, it has whiled away several otherwise weary hours & I have enjoyed it exceedingly."

At the end of November, Lu had a birthday. It was only the year before that she had waited anxiously to turn thirty so she could enlist in the army. This year's birthday proved to be a disappointment. "Was 31 on the 29th, only one or two presents & a dull day as usual." Christmas proved to be an even bigger disappointment.

Or so she thought. There was one gift, but she wouldn't realize it until many years later when she came across a diary entry she had written in 1863 about *Hospital Sketches*. Now mature from all her life experiences, she wrote to her younger self: "Short-sighted, Louisa! Little did you dream that...you [were] to make your fortune a few years later. The 'Sketches' never made much money, but showed me 'my style,' & taking the hint I went where glory waited me."

Part Two

WHERE GLORY WAITS

Chapter 11

UNFULFILLED DESTINY

November 1865, La Tour de Peilz, Switzerland
Seven months after the end of the Civil War

O N A WINDY NOVEMBER MORNING IN THE SMALL SWISS village of La Tour de Peilz, Lu was in the dining room of the Pension Victoria, an elegant boardinghouse on the shores of Lake Geneva. Although she was eating breakfast by herself, Lu wasn't traveling through Europe alone. About three months ago, in July, William Weld, a shipping, railroad, and real estate tycoon, had hired Lu to travel with his invalid daughter, Anna, as her companion.

"Hearing that I was something of a nurse & wanted to travel [he] proposed my going. . . . I agreed though I had my doubts, but every one said 'Go,' so after a week of work & worry I did," Lu recorded in her journal.

But Lu was still having second thoughts about the trip. "I missed my freedom & grew very tired of the daily worry which I had to go through," Lu revealed.

Thirty-year-old Anna Weld wasn't an easy patient to take care of, and it wasn't clear what exactly ailed her, but the doctors in Europe were trying to cure her. Lu and Anna had spent the summer in Schwalbach, a German town famous for its bubbling mineral water, some of which tasted like wine. Anna had been under the care of Dr. Adolph Genth, the author of *The Iron Waters of Schwalbach*. Lu was familiar with the water cure. Her mother, Abba, had left the family and worked briefly in Maine as the matron of a water cure spa and believed in its effectiveness. It was a very popular treatment in New England and went hand-in-hand with developing women's rights.

Many water cure spas actively recruited female workers and doctors (of which there weren't many), so their female patients would feel comfortable receiving treatment, especially relating to pregnancy, menstruation, and chronic ailments that male doctors often dismissed as "female complaints." The cure involved wrapping the patient in a wet sheet for a few hours so she would sweat, then she was plunged into cold water. The patient was also prescribed long walks, fresh air, rest, bathing, and eight glasses of water a day.

Lu found life at Schwalbach boring. "We walked a little, talked a little, bathed, & rode a little, worried a good deal, & I grubbed away at French with no master & small success . . . rather dull days bathing, walking, & quiddling about," she recounted.

The good news was the doctor thought Anna's condition had improved, even though she still complained and fussed. "I tried my best to suit & serve her," Lu wrote. "But don't think I did so very well, yet many would have done still worse I fancy, for hers is a very hard case to manage & needs patience & wisdom of an angel."

Lu understood illness firsthand, both as a patient and nurse, and she was sympathetic. But she had also experienced firsthand the horrors of war, and, like the men she had nursed, Lu had used all her strength trying to fight her way back from the brink of death. So it was difficult for her to relate to Anna's fragility, which many considered an attractive feminine quality. But Lu didn't. Like many feminists of the time, Lu believed that most female fragility was the result of society's rules, restricting women from exercise, such as running, and expecting them to wear uncomfortable clothes. The corset was the biggest offender, which was not only tight and painful but made breathing and physical exertion difficult. Lu believed that fragility kept women from fully participating in life.

Compounding Lu and Anna's differences were their lots in life. In Lu's family, the burden of taking care of everyone fell on her, especially because her father had recently lost his job as the superintendent of the Concord schools. In stark contrast, Anna, who was a thirty-year-old spinster, was a daddy's girl. She had been taken care of her whole life, showered in luxury with no financial worries or any obligation to work—a foreign concept, so to speak, for Lu.

Lu had been worried about putting her writing career on hold while she traveled, especially because she was gaining momentum. After the critical success of *Hospital Sketches*, her love-triangle romance *Moods* was published. Lu had mixed feelings about it. "The book was hastily got out, but on the whole suited me. . . . For a week wherever I went I saw, heard, & talked 'Moods,'" Lu chronicled. "Found people laughing or crying over it, & was continually told how well it was going, how much it was liked, how fine a thing I'd done. I was glad but not proud, I think, for it has always seemed as if 'Moods' grew in spite of me, & that I had little to do with it except to put into words the thoughts that would not let me rest until I had."

After *Moods* was published, Lu tried to work on her other novel in progress, *Success* (later titled *Work*), but she abandoned it to write more "blood and thunder" tales. "Being tired of novels, I soon dropped it & fell back on rubbishy tales, for they pay best & I can't afford to starve on praise, when sensation stories are written in half the time & keep the family cosy," Lu wrote.

But when she was offered the chance to travel to Europe, a lifelong dream, her family insisted that she should go. Lu reasoned that the life experience, like her time at the Union Hotel Hospital, would give her material for more stories, so she was writing down everything in her pocket diary and letters home.

Before leaving Schwalbach, Lu had finally received her first letter from home. She was thrilled that they missed her. "All is happy & well, thank God!" she noted in her journal. "It touched & pleased me very much to see how they missed me, thought of me, & and longed to have me back. Every little thing I ever did for them is now so tenderly & gratefully remembered, & my absence seems to have left so large a gap that I begin to realize how much I am to them in spite of all my faults."

Soon after receiving the letter, Lu and Anna left Schwalbach and traveled through Germany, stopping in the charming Heidelburg, the fashionable Baden Baden, the lovely Lausanne, before finally reaching La Tour de la Peilz. But Lu quickly realized she didn't like it at the Pension Victoria. It wasn't the accommodations. The rooms were comfortable, the food was good, and the setting was beautiful, with a view of the glittering lake surrounded by snow-capped mountains. It was the guests who were disagreeable, specifically the Polk family from Maury County, Tennessee.

Although the South had lost the Civil War with the fall of Richmond and the surrender of General Robert E. Lee, the Confederacy's most respected commander, a few days later, it was followed by the assassination of President Lincoln. The conflict lived on, and Lu was discovering firsthand that the hateful bitterness between both sides endured even on the other side of the world.

At dinner, the first day Lu and Anna were at the Pension Victoria, someone asked them where they were from. "Boston, Massachusetts," Lu replied. She looked around the long table and noticed a once-handsome, thin, sallow man with gray hair and a mustache glowering at her. And so were his wife and daughter.

Lu learned that the man was Colonel Andrew J. Polk, one of the wealthiest plantation owners in the state of Tennessee. He had fought for the Confederate army and been badly wounded, and one of his brothers had been killed. When the Yankees arrived in Tennessee, Colonel Polk and his family had fled their princely eighteen-room brick mansion situated on a thousand acres of fertile farmland and equipped with brick barns, brick outbuildings, and a glass greenhouse covering two acres. Their five hundred slaves had also fled, to freedom.

"Thoroughly beaten, I could not wonder that we were unwelcome neighbors," Lu penned. "And [I] tried not to show any ungenerous exultation, though I must confess the blood of a born abolitionist simmered—not to say boiled—when I heard the tales they told, [and] found myself insulted daily."

In the evenings, Colonel Polk played cards with the other guests while drinking too much brandy. His wife, Rebecca, heiress to an iron fortune that had used slave labor, complained about the hardships and ill health her husband had suffered from the Civil War. She told stories about the Union soldiers, calling them barbaric cowards, and how their slaves had been happy and loyal, but the Yankees had forced them away. She believed their slaves were longing for their "master" to return.

Her husband boasted that he'd given his slaves a church. "A church to Almighty God, sir," he exclaimed with a Southern drawl. "And it was a rare sport to see 'em preaching and praying. I used to take my friends down to enjoy the fun. I let 'em marry, too, and gave away the bride myself. You'd roar to see 'em jump the broomstick." Polk didn't mention that it was his slaves who had dug the clay, kilned the bricks, cut the wood, and built the church.

Polk also made sure Lu heard him laugh about a wounded Union soldier who was taken prisoner. Like Lu's second-favorite patient, Baby B., his arm was shattered from a bullet and needed to be amputated. But the Confederate surgeon amputated his leg instead of his arm, so he could never fight again.

Interestingly, Colonel Polk's cousin was the eleventh president of the United States, James Polk, who was considered the last strong president before Abraham Lincoln took office. Polk had been elected on the platform of "manifest destiny"—westward expansion across the continent. During Polk's presidency, he delivered on his promise, and the United States grew by one-third, adding Texas, New Mexico, Arizona, Colorado, Nevada, Utah, Wyoming, California, and the Oregon Territory. But the expansion of the country also ignited the conflict over the expansion of slavery, effectively dividing the country and driving it to war.

At the Pension Victoria, the hostility seethed between Lu and the Polks, and Lu was shocked that the other guests, who hailed from other countries, sympathized with the Polks. Some, like the English, claimed neutrality, a Frenchman just shrugged his shoulders, and two ladies from Scotland advised Lu to be careful, warning her that Colonel Polk was a desperate and, therefore, dangerous man. Lu didn't try to provoke the Polks intentionally, but when she learned that they were traveling with a black nurse named Betty who was once their slave, she always made a point of acknowledging her. Lu stood firm in her belief that all humans deserve equal rights.

BUT ON this windy November morning, while Lu was eating her breakfast, her dislike for the Pension Victoria was about to change when the outside door opened, and a cold draft blew through the dining room. Lu was sitting at the long dining room table in her assigned seat by the stove, and when the icy breeze barely cut through the blazing heat radiating in her corner, she heard someone cough. Lu recognized the low hollow cough from her nursing experience. It was the sound of a death knell.

Lu looked over in the direction of the continued coughing, and she saw a new guest stand up from his assigned seat by the door. While he went to shut the door, Lu noticed he was tall with a thin and intelligent-looking face and expressive blue eyes. Several more times the door was left open by a boarder, and he got up to shut it. And more than once, Lu saw him shiver and cast a wistful glance at her assigned seat near the warm stove. "That boy is sick and needs care. I must see to him," Lu thought to herself.

Lu stood up from her table, and he gave her a little bow while opening the door for her. Lu bowed her head in response, then went to find the landlady and have their assigned seats switched. That evening at dinner when Lu looked over, she saw him looking cozy by the warm stove. He thanked her with a smile and a look of gratitude. Their seats were too far apart to talk much, so he filled his glass, bowed to Lu, and said in French, "I drink the good health to mademoiselle."

Lu returned the good wish to him, and he smiled but shook his head. She noticed a sudden shadow darken his expression, and she knew her words meant more to him than she had first realized. After dinner, he followed her into the living room and thanked her in English. "So simple, frank and grateful was he," Lu wrote, "that in half an hour he had told me his story, and I felt a friendly interest in him."

His name was Ladislas "Laddie" Weisneiwsky. He was a twenty-year-old Polish musician, and he had lost everything— his parents, home, fortune, country, and health—in the rebellion against Russian rule in Poland. "With his fellow students he had fought through the last outbreak, been imprisoned, and while there, had learned his parents were killed in a cold-blooded massacre, where five hundred Poles were shot down for singing their national hymn in the market-place," Lu recounted.

While in prison, Laddie had become ill with tuberculosis, which was most likely a death sentence, and, for reasons unknown, he was released. But he was banished from Poland for refusing to swear his allegiance to Russia. So he made his way to Germany a year ago, then to Switzerland, "and manfully began the hard fight for life," Lu wrote. Laddie told Lu that in the springtime he wanted to move to Paris, where two of his friends were living and where he hoped to find work teaching music. This sparked Lu's curiosity about his talent.

"Play me the forbidden hymn," Lu said.

Laddie hesitated, then scanned the room, prompting Lu to ask who he was looking for.

"I look to see if the baron is here," Laddie said in broken English, which Lu noted was the prettiest she'd ever heard. "He is Russian, and to him my national air will not be pleasing."

"Then play it," Lu said. "He dare not forbid you here, and I should rather enjoy that little insult to your bitter enemy."

"Ah, mademoiselle," he said. "It is true we are enemies, but we are also gentlemen."

Lu thanked him "for giving me a lesson in real politeness which I did not forget."

Since the Russian baron wasn't there, Laddie played for her, singing his national hymn enthusiastically despite his weak lungs. "From that evening we were fast friends," Lu explained. "For the memory of certain dear lads at home made my heart warm to this lonely boy, who gave me in return the most grateful affection and respect."

Laddie fit the type of man Lu was attracted to, and he shared qualities with her "prince of patients," John Suhre—tall, expressive eyes, noble, courageous, willing to give his life for a cause he believed in, injured lungs, someone who needed to be taken care of, and, most importantly, unavailable. Lu was smitten, and she liked Laddie even more when he took her side in her conflict with the Polks. In fact, everyone was about to change their minds and take Lu's side.

ONE DAY the Polks's nurse, Betty, knocked on Lu's door. Lu ushered Betty inside, where she saw the two "neutral" Englishwomen.

The four of them began talking, and Betty told them about herself, describing "her wrongs with the simple eloquence of truth." The two women from England began to cry and asked Betty whether it was true what Mrs. Polk said, that the slaves were forced away and longed to have their master back. Betty told them no, it wasn't, thanking God and the Yankees.

Worried that Mrs. Polk was telling more lies, they asked Betty whether she was free. Betty nodded her head but told them Mrs. Polk figured Betty wouldn't run off while they were in Europe. Betty explained she was biding her time. Once her feet touched American soil, she was leaving the Polks.

The English were no longer neutral and felt compelled to whisper Betty's story to the other guests, revealing the Polks's lies. To Lu's satisfaction, "The tables were completely turned and the North won the day again."

It was another blustery day on Lake Geneva when Lu's thirty-third birthday arrived on November 29. She thought of her father, who was turning sixty-six, and how she would miss the little ceremony her family always had on their shared birthday. But Lu was having one of the best birthday celebrations ever.

Anna had given her a pretty painting, and Laddie had promised Lu the notes of the Polish National Hymn along with wishing her "all good & happiness on earth & a high place in Heaven as my reward." Lu expressed her feelings in her journal: "It was a wild, windy day, very like me in its fitful changes of sunshine & shade. Usually I am sad on my birthday, but not this time, for though nothing very pleasant happened I was happy & hopeful & enjoyed everything with unusual relish."

Since Laddie's arrival, they had spent a lot of time together. He was teaching her French, and she was teaching him English. He also entertained everyone, playing the piano enthusiastically and bringing down the house. Other times, Lu and Laddie sailed and walked the shores of Lake Geneva, sharing confidences, and every night he presented her with a winter rose at dinner. He also slipped little notes with funny illustrations under her door, calling them chapters of a great history that they were writing together.

"A little romance with L[adislas] W[eisneiwsky]," Lu confided in her journal in December. But, later, Lu crossed out the rest of the entry, her pen scratching so fiercely that she destroyed the paper.

A week after Lu's birthday, on December 6, Anna and Lu left the Pension Victoria and traveled to Nice, where Anna wanted to spend the winter. Laddie went to see them off. There were tears in his eyes as he kissed both Anna and Lu's hands and said, "I do not say adieu but *au revoir*." For Lu, it wasn't good-bye. She would meet him again in Paris. Alone.

A FEW WEEKS later, on Christmas day in 1865, Lu was stuck in her hotel room. The window was open, and she could see that the roses were blooming and the people outside seemed jolly, but, for Lu, the day was dull. Most days were dull for Lu, and she was homesick as well. "Very tired of doing nothing pleasant or interesting," Lu recorded in her journal.

When they first arrived in the seacoast town on the French Riviera, Lu described Nice as "lovely," "pleasant," and "beautiful." A horse-drawn carriage would take them for a ride along the wide Promenade des Anglais, which was dotted with palm trees, luxury hotels, shops, castles, a lighthouse, and impeccably dressed people in the latest fashions. But, soon after their arrival, Anna became ill. A famous doctor was called, and he was trying to cure her with medicine, but she wasn't improving.

Anna was also upset about Laddie. In response, Lu wrote a cryptic entry in her journal, leading some scholars to wonder whether a love triangle had developed. Lu noted, "Anna was troubled about Laddie who was in a despairing state of mind. I could not advise them [which she later crossed out and wrote 'him,' then crossed it out] to be happy as they desired, so every-thing went wrong & both worried."

No further explanation was given, but Lu's actions give some insight. A month later, in February, after Anna sent the famous doctor away, she started to feel much better. And Lu decided she was going to quit, writing, "My time is too valuable to be spent fussing over cushions & carrying shawls. I'm rather fond of her but she wears upon me & we are best apart."

On the first day of May 1866, Lu left Anna. She felt "as happy as a freed bird. Anna cried & seemed to feel badly, but it was best to part, & having come to that conclusion long ago I never changed my mind, but made her as comfortable as I could with a maid & companion & then turned my face toward home rejoicing."

On her journey home, Lu made a stop—Paris. When she stepped off the train, she found Laddie waiting for her at the station. His face was beaming, and he grasped her hands in his. Lu laughed, feeling that Paris was almost as good as home.

"You are better?" Lu asked.

"I truly hope so," he said. "The winter was good to me and I cough less. It is small hope, but I do not enlarge my fear by a sad face."

Lu revealed in her journal that she spent a "very charming" two weeks with Laddie in Paris. He was her tour guide, showing her all the sights she wanted to see. He helped her pick out a new bonnet, took strolls with her through Luxembourg Garden, and in the evenings played music for her. On May 17, Lu reluctantly started on her journey home. The details are general and vague in her journal, giving no indication whether he was her lover. But, later, Lu went back to the entry in her journal for December, and on the torn piece of paper she wrote, "couldn't be."

ALTHOUGH LU didn't know it at the time, her love for Laddie was going to live on forever not only in her heart but also in her writing. And, in the stories that she would write for publication about her time with Laddie, she would make the point that he was like a son to her. But Lu didn't describe their friendship like that in her personal journal. Later in life, Lu would confide to a friend in a letter about lost love and unfulfilled destiny.

"If in my present life if I love one person truly, no matter who it is, I believe that we meet somewhere again, though where or how I don't know or care, for genuine love is immortal."

Chapter 12

THE CHARIOT OF GLORY

May 1868, Concord, Massachusetts
Two years later

M R. NILES WANTS A *GIRLS'* STORY," LU WROTE IN HER diary.

Thomas Niles worked for Roberts Brothers, the company that wanted to publish *Hospital Sketches*, but Lu had turned him down, preferring to publish with James Redpath. This wasn't the first time that Mr. Niles had asked Lu to write a girls' story. He first asked eight months earlier, and Lu told him she'd try. But Lu decided she didn't like writing for girls, and she put it aside, until Mr. Niles asked her again.

Despite having published *Success* (later called *Work*), and earning more money for her short stories, Lu still scrambled to make enough income to support her family. When Lu returned home from Europe, she had found that her family was in even more debt. "The money-maker was away," Lu wrote. But she found more stories to tell after her trip and got busy writing. "Got to work...for bills accumulate and worry me," Lu explained. "I dread debt more than anything."

After her father had lost his job as superintendent of the Concord school, Bronson also got serious about finishing his manuscript, *Tablets*, in which he was trying to express his philosophical ideology. But he was a better talker than writer. And even though Bronson's fame as a philosopher was growing—he was referred to by this time as "Emerson's master" and the "Sage of Concord"—only one publisher was interested in his manuscript. It was Mr. Niles of Roberts Brothers. But Mr. Niles would only publish it if Lu would write a girls' story. Otherwise, Bronson's earning prospects were slim. Although he still toured the country giving lectures, he didn't make much money from it.

Bronson felt regret, knowing it was his cross to bear that he couldn't support his family: "Alas! I wish, for her [my wife's] sake and my children's, I could have a pair of profitable hands and marketable wits. But no!...and I must pay the cost of such gifts as I have by the lack of such as I have not, in something like dependence on others."

The strain and burden of financial hardship over the years had taken a toll on Lu's mother, who was now sixty-seven years old and in poor health. Lu believed she was in a decline. "I never expect to see the strong, energetic Marmee of old times, but, thank the Lord! she is still here, though pale and weak, quiet and sad," Lu wrote. "All her fine hair is gone, and face full of wrinkles, bowed back, and every sign of age. Life has been hard for her, and she so brave, so glad to spend herself for others. Now we must live for her."

Lu wanted this year to be different and was more determined than ever to realize her dream of supporting her family and being independent. So, she took another stab at the "girls' story," albeit reluctantly. "I begin 'Little Women.'...I plod away, though

I don't enjoy this sort of thing," Lu confessed. "Never liked girls or knew many, except my sisters, but our queer plays and experiences may prove interesting, though I doubt it."

Drawing on her early life experiences, Lu stuck to the facts but changed the time, place, and names. She set her story during the Civil War, now three years over, and each family member was a character. Lu was Jo. Her older sister, Anna, was Meg. Her younger sister, May, was Amy. And Lu wrote about her sister, Lizzie, as Beth. Although Julian Hawthorne would believe the character Laurie was based on him, he was really inspired by her love of Laddie.

In her book, Lu also softened the grim reality of her family's poverty and focused on their affection and love for one another without idealizing the girls. She wanted them to talk and act like real girls. Lu's flair for humor shone throughout the book.

While writing about her sister Beth's death, Lu was able to convey how caring for someone who is terminally ill can be a painfully harsh but valuable lesson in life that matures the caretaker, like Jo in the book. This was something Lu had learned from loving John Suhre and watching him die at the Union Hotel Hospital.

The next month, in June, Lu sent Mr. Niles twelve chapters of *Little Women*. "He thought it *dull*, so do I," Lu grumbled. But she kept working on it. Mr. Niles told her there was a great need for "lively, simple books" for girls, and Lu hoped she could meet that need. Wrapped in her glory cloak, Lu worked in her "vortex," barely leaving her desk and hardly eating or sleeping.

On July 15, she finished and sent her manuscript to Mr. Niles. Lu had written 402 pages but to her detriment. "Very tired, head full of pain from overwork, and heart heavy about Marmee, who is growing feeble," Lu wrote.

The following month, Mr. Niles made an offer on *Little Women* and advised Lu to keep the copyright. On August 26, he sent her the page proofs to read and correct before the final printing. When Lu read through it, she was surprised. "It reads better than I expected. Not a bit sensational, but simple and true, for we really lived most of it; and if it succeeds that will be the reason of it." She didn't realize she had written her masterpiece.

About a month later, on September 30, *Little Women* was released. A month after that, Lu found out that her book was selling better than expected. "Saw Mr. Niles....[H]e gave me good news....First edition gone and more called for....Mr. Niles wants a second volume. Pleasant notices and letters arrive, and much interest in my little women, who seem to find friends by their truth to life, as I hoped."

The instant success of *Little Women* inspired Lu to start writing the second volume the very next day. There was one pressing question she needed to answer in the sequel. Who was Jo going to marry? In nearly all the letters she received, the readers wanted Jo to marry Laurie. Lu was perturbed. "Girls write to ask who the little women marry, as if that was the only end and aim of a woman's life. I won't marry Jo to Laurie to please any one."

And she didn't.

"'Jo' should have remained a literary spinster," Lu asserted. "But so many enthusiastic young ladies wrote to me clamorously demanding that she should marry Laurie, *or* somebody, that I didn't dare to refuse & out of perversity went & made a funny match for her. I expect vials of wrath to be poured upon my head, but rather enjoy the prospect."

Lu's goal was to write a chapter a day. She wanted to finish by the end of November. "I am so full of my work, I can't stop to eat or sleep, or for anything but a daily run."

On November 29, Lu turned thirty-six years old. She spent it alone, busy writing. The only present she received was from her father. He had given her a copy of his recently published book, *Tablets*. "I never seem to have many presents, as some do, though I give a good many," Lu noted. "That is best perhaps, and makes a gift precious when it does come."

On New Year's Day 1869, Lu delivered the final manuscript to her publisher. That month, she paid off her family's seemingly never-ending debt. "Paid up all the debts, thank the Lord!—every penny that money can pay,—and now I feel as if I could die in peace," Lu exclaimed proudly. "My dream is beginning to come true, and if my head holds out I'll do all I once hoped to do."

In April when the sequel to *Little Women* came out, it was a big success, receiving more good reviews and brisk sales. Mr. Niles wanted Lu to write another book, but she didn't think she could do it. At least not yet. Lu's health was failing. She wrote that she felt "quite used up. Don't care for myself, as rest is heavenly even with pain, but the family seems so panic-stricken and helpless when I break down, that I try to keep the mill going." Ever since her bout with typhoid pneumonia, Lu's head pounded, she felt dizzy, her body ached, and a butterfly rash bloomed across her face. The doctors believed she was suffering from acute mercury poisoning, from the calomel Dr. Stipp had prescribed. (Modern doctors postulate the calomel may have triggered lupus, an auto-immune disease, for which there is no cure.) It would ultimately shorten her life.

In August 1869, with the success of parts 1 and 2 of *Little Women*, she had more than $1,000 for a rainy day after she had paid off all her family's bills. "With that thought I can bear neuralgia gayly," Lu wrote.

In October, Lu was trying to write her next book, *Old-Fashioned Girl*, but she was so sick, she couldn't even speak. She went to the doctor every day, and he burned her windpipe with a caustic as a remedy. Despite her illness, Lu would finish the book with her "left hand in a sling, one foot up, head aching, and no voice." She believed that she certainly earned her living by the sweat of her brow.

The sweat of her brow paid off in December 1869, when Lu finally had something to celebrate on Christmas. A letter from her publisher arrived with a royalty check for $2,500. "Many thanks for the check which made my Christmas an unusually merry one," Lu wrote to her publisher. "After toiling so many years along the up-hill road, always a hard one to women writers, it is peculiarly grateful to me to find the way growing easier at last, with pleasant little surprises blossoming on either side, and the rough places made smooth by courtesy and kindness of those who have proved themselves 'friends' as well as 'publishers.'"

Fame and fortune were finally hers. Lu's "dull book" was the first golden egg, and she achieved her goal of taking care of her family and giving them every comfort. Fans were knocking on her front door, and Lu found herself acting like her neighbor, Nathaniel Hawthorne, scurrying away, afraid someone would spot her. Although Lu didn't enjoy the spotlight, her father did. "I am introduced as the father of Little Women, and am riding in the Chariot of Glory wherever I go," he noted in his journal. Later, he would travel the country giving lectures and billing himself as the "Gifted Sire of Louisa M. Alcott! Authoress of Little Women." The venues were sold out, jammed with people eager to hear him speak. Finally.

ALTHOUGH LU never dreamed that her work would endure for generations and that her "girls' book" would be treasured by readers all over the world, she had dared to dream of success. "As a poor, proud, struggling girl I held to the belief that if I *deserved* success it would surely come so long as my ambition was not for selfish ends but for my dear family," Lu confided to a friend. "And it did come, far more fully than I ever hoped or dreamed, though youth, health and many hopes went to earn it."

Epilogue

STILL ON THE FRONT LINES

July 1879, Concord, Massachusetts
Ten years later

THE SUMMER SKY WAS NEARLY FREE OF CLOUDS, AND the heat was, surprisingly, not oppressive in the small village of Concord in July 1879. This was good news for seventy-nine-year-old Bronson Alcott, who had opened his School of Philosophy and was holding "conversations" in his study at Orchard House. The thirty "budding philosophers" were comfortable as they listened to different lectures each morning and spent their free time visiting the sights, such as Walden Woods and Pond.

"He has *his* dream realized at last & is in glory with plenty of talk to swim in," Lu wrote in her journal. "People will laugh but will enjoy some thing new in this dull old town."

Forty-six-year-old Lu was also trying to stir up interest in something new in Concord. Lu wanted women to have the right to vote, and if she succeeded, Lu would realize a dream that she had shared with her beloved mother. Abba herself had petitioned, more than once, for women's rights, stating, "If [women] can emancipate the slave... they must work out their

193

own emancipation. They [women] must help make the Laws, Be educated as Jurists, Drs. Divines, Artists, Bankers. It will occupy and give dignity to their minds."

Two years earlier, Abba had died in Lu's arms from congestive heart failure, her dream still unrealized. Abba's death was a terrible loss for Lu, who was suffering from chronic physical pain from her own poor health. Lu revealed in her journal that "a great warmth seems gone out of life, and there is no motive to go on now. My only comfort is that I *could* make her last years comfortable, and lift off the burden she had carried so bravely all these years. She was so loyal, tender, and true; life was hard for her, and no one understood all she had to bear but we, her children."

To help manage her grief, Lu focused her mind and energy on women's suffrage, which, as her mother had noted in her journal, the town of Concord was "wonderfully indifferent to." But Lu always liked a challenge, and in the face of opposition she was always more determined. "I like to help women help themselves," Lu explained. "As that is, in my opinion, the best way to settle the woman question. Whatever we can do and do well we have a right to, and I don't think any one will deny us."

In 1877, the New England Woman Suffrage Association campaigned to allow women to vote in local town meetings on the two issues women were considered experts on—children and education. Their goal was to start on the local level to open the door for state and federal elections. Massachusetts voted to pass the measure.

To ignite interest, Lu held meetings at her home. At the first meeting, only twelve women were expected, but twenty-five showed up. "Very informal meetings, where we met and talked over the matter, asked questions, compared notes and got ready to go and register," Lu reported.

Lu was leading by example. On July 23, one week after Bronson opened his School of Philosophy, Lu hurried down to the Town Hall and was the first woman to register her name as a voter in Concord. But not everyone from her meetings showed up. "I am ashamed to say that out of a hundred women who pay taxes on property in Concord, only seven have as yet registered... [a] very poor record for a town which ought to lead if it really possesses all the intelligence claimed for it," she wrote.

But it wasn't too late, and in August Lu rode about town in her horse and carriage, knocking on doors and encouraging women to attend her suffrage meeting. "So hard to move people out of old ruts," she stated.

Despite some of the apathy, Bronson encouraged and fully supported Lu's involvement, revealing in his journal, "I have words in favor of Woman Suffrage. I am gratified in the fact that my daughters are loyal to their sex and to their sainted mother, who, had she survived, would have been the first to have taken them to the polls."

By the time the town election arrived on March 29, 1880, twenty-eight women had registered to vote. But only twenty, including Lu, showed up. The no-shows were generally over-whelmed with domestic chores and child-care responsibilities. Nevertheless, the registered women voters who had arrived, many with their husbands, fathers, and brothers, were all in good spirits.

When the time came to vote for the new school committee, the moderator announced that the women would vote first—thanks to Bronson's suggestion. No one objected, and the women made a line, cast their votes, and went quietly back to their seats. The men watched in solemn silence.

"No bolt fell on our audacious heads, no earthquake shook the town, but a pleasing surprise created a general outbreak of laughter and applause," Lu recounted.

While everyone was still laughing, the judge, who was overseeing the voting, told the men that the polls were closed. Lu thought he was joking, but he wasn't. She noticed that some of the men "looked disturbed at being deprived of their rights." Lu thought it was perfectly fair because the women weren't allowed to voice their opinions on any other issue.

One man remarked that it didn't matter whether the men voted anyway because the women all voted just as their husbands, fathers, and brothers would have voted, implying that they couldn't think for themselves. Lu took offense to his remark but was satisfied with the election.

"We elected a good school committee," Lu stated firmly.

At five o'clock, the wives left the Town Hall and hurried home to make tea for their husbands. Lu was feeling hopeful, predicting that, in the following year, more women would turn out to vote. "The ice is broken. . . . [I]t is the first step that counts," Lu wrote. "And when the timid or indifferent . . . see that we still live, they will venture to express publicly the opinions they held or have lately learned to respect and believe."

ON AUGUST 18, 1920, the Nineteenth Amendment to the US Constitution was finally ratified, giving women the right to vote in state and federal elections. It was forty years after Lu had cast her vote, taking the first step to drive this important change.

If I can do no more, let my name stand among those who are willing to bear ridicule and reproach for the truth's sake, and so earn some right to rejoice when the victory is won. Most heartily for woman's suffrage and all other reforms.

Louisa May Alcott

ACKNOWLEDGMENTS

It has been a real pleasure for me to research and write about Louisa May Alcott, a dynamic woman whose spitfire spirit leaps off the pages of her journals and letters. Deepest thanks to Stephanie Knapp for her enthusiasm, clear vision, and guidance as we navigated the editorial waters to reveal a little-known part of Lu's life story. Many thanks to Holly Rubino for her careful reading of the manuscript and her challenging questions. My heartfelt thanks to Jessica Regel for her encouragement and enthusiasm over the years (and for the title of this book). A big thank you to Amber Morris for the smooth transitions in the editorial production process and to Carrie Watterson and her fine-tuned editing pen.

I also want to thank the librarians, archivists, and research assistants who helped me uncover unpublished letters that were used to develop different aspects of Lu's experience as a Civil War nurse: Malia Ebel of the New Hampshire Historical Society, Sabina Beauchard of the Massachusetts Historical Society, Girish Naik of Harvard University, and Kimberly Reynolds of the Boston Public Library.

My love and thanks to my husband, Todd, who always tells me, "You can do it!"

SOURCE NOTES

Introduction: The Heroine's Journey

"My life is one of daily protest": Abigail May Alcott, April 28, 1851, *My Heart Is Boundless: Writings of Abigail May Alcott, Louisa's Mother*, ed. Eve LaPlante (New York: Free Press, 2012), 181.

"radical manifesto": Alison Lurie, "She Had It All," *New York Review of Books* 42, no. 4 (March 2, 1995): 5.

Chapter 1: Wayward Daughter

"poor as rats": Louisa May Alcott, [Notes and Memoranda, 1851], *The Journals of Louisa May Alcott*, ed. Joel Myerson and Daniel Shealy (Athens: University of Georgia Press), 65. [Hereafter LMA, *The Journals*.]

"We are used to hard times": Louisa May Alcott, December 1860, LMA, *The Journals*, 101.

"A most uncommon fit of generosity": Ibid., 103.

"more patch and tear than gown": Ibid.

"We supplied him with the means": Bronson Alcott, February 9, 1847, *The Journals of Bronson Alcott*, ed. Odell Shepard (Boston: Little, Brown, 1938), 190.

"Glad I have lived to see": LMA, *The Journals*, 95.

"I'm a better patriot": Ibid., 101.

"If I look in my glass": Ibid., 61.

"I went to a barber": Maria S. Porter, "Recollections of Louisa May Alcott," *New England Magazine* 6, no. 1 (March 1892): 5–6.

"That was not the first time": Ibid., 6.

"Philosophers are always poor": LMA, *The Journals*, 84.

SOURCE NOTES

"the most transcendental of the Transcendentalists": Allen Johnson, ed., *Dictionary of American Biography* (New York: Charles Scribner's Sons, 1928), 139.

"a fanatic in belief": Clara Gowing, *The Alcotts as I Knew Them* (Boston: C. M. Clark, 1909), 1.

"trailing clouds of glory": Harriet Reisen, *Louisa May Alcott: The Woman Behind "Little Women"* (New York: Picador, 2009), 20. From William Wordsworth's "Ode: Intimations of Immortality from Recollections of Early Childhood."

"Father, mother, sister, objects": Honoré Willsie Morrow, *The Father of Little Women* (Boston: Little, Brown, 1927), 157.

"wild exuberance": Reisen, *Louisa May Alcott*, 33.

"I do not believe in": Morrow, *The Father of Little Women*, 152.

"She listened to what": Ibid.

"She only looks toward": Ibid., 155.

"the worst child ever known": Louisa May Alcott, *Aunt Jo's Scrap-Bag* (Boston: Roberts Brothers, 1872), 6.

"Ever your loving demon": John Matteson, "Little Woman: The Devilish, Dutiful Daughter Louisa May Alcott," *Humanities* 30, no. 6 (November/December 2009), accessed November 2016, https://www.neh.gov/humanities/2009/novemberdecember/feature/little-woman.

"No animal substances": Gowing, *The Alcotts as I Knew Them*, 60–61.

"Circumstances most cruelly drive": Abba May Alcott, November 29, 1842, *The Journals of Bronson Alcott*, 148.

"More people coming to live with us": Louisa May Alcott, *Louisa May Alcott: Her Life, Letters, and Journals*, ed. Ednah Dow Cheney (Carlisle, MA: Applewood Books, 1889), 43–44.

"He was very strict": Gowing, *The Alcotts as I Knew Them*, 61–62.

"I was very unhappy": Alcott, *Louisa May Alcott: Her Life, Letters, and Journals*, 39.

"The arrangements here [at Fruitlands]": Reisen, *Louisa May Alcott*, 104.

"I do not allow myself": Ibid., 100.

"No one will employ him": Riesen, Ibid., 62.

"Don't distress yourself": John Matteson, *Eden's Outcasts: The Story of Louisa May Alcott and Her Father* (New York: W. W. Norton, 2007), 5.

SOURCE NOTES

"*He is moderate, I am impetuous*": Reisen, *Louisa May Alcott*, 17.

"*Wife, children, and friends are less*": Abba Alcott, April 1, 1842, *The Journals of Bronson Alcott*, 141.

"*It is this dependence on others*": Abigail May Alcott, April 4, 1841, *My Heart Is Boundless*, 88.

"*I have no accomplishments*": Ibid.

"*She always did what came*": LMA, *The Journals*, 67.

"*a shelter for lost girls*": Ibid.

"*It was not fit work*": Ibid.

"*My girls* shall *have trades*": Abigail May Alcott, *My Heart Is Boundless*, 88.

"*To the great dismay of the neighbors' hens*": Alcott, *Louisa May Alcott: Her Life, Letters, and Journals*, 30.

"*I have made a plan*": Ibid., 48.

"*be a help and a comfort*": Ibid.

"*My quick tongue is always*": LMA, *The Journals*, 61–62.

"*I will do something*": Daniel Shealy, ed., *Alcott in Her Own Time: A Biographical Chronicle of Her Life, Drawn from Recollections, Interviews, and Memoirs by Family, Friends, and Associates* (Iowa City: University of Iowa Press, 2005), 37.

"*My book came out*": Alcott, *Louisa May Alcott: Her Life, Letters, and Journals*, 80.

"*After ten years of hard climbing*": Ibid., 121.

"*I'd rather be a free spinster*": Ibid., 122.

"*I often think what a hard life*": Ibid., 62.

"*I corked up my inkstand*": Ibid., 124.

"*It seems to me*": Morrow, *The Father of Little Women*, 271.

"*A hard thing to hear*": Alcott, *Louisa May Alcott: Her Life, Letters, and Journals*, 96.

"*My dear Beth [Lizzie] died*": Ibid., 97.

"*She is well at last*": Louisa May Alcott to Eliza Wells, March 19, 1858, *The Selected Letters of Louisa May Alcott*, ed. Joel Myerson and Daniel Shealy (Athens: University of Georgia Press, 1995), 32. [Hereafter LMA, *Letters*.]

"*Wonder if I ought not be a nurse*": Alcott, *Louisa May Alcott: Her Life, Letters, and Journals*, 103.

SOURCE NOTES

Chapter 2: Stitches

"The Confederate Traitors": "The New York Press upon the War," *Evening Star*, April 17, 1861, 1.

"The call for troops": Ibid.

"Concord had raised $4,000": Ellen Emerson to Edward Emerson, April 19, 1861, *The Letters of Ellen Tucker Emerson*, 2 vols., ed. Edith E. W. Gregg (Kent, OH: Kent State University Press, 1982), 1:242.

"kindled a patriotic rage": "The New York Press upon the War," 1.

"I long to be a man": LMA, *The Journals*, 105.

"A busy time getting them ready": Ibid.

"At the station the scene": Ibid.

"John Brown's daughters came to board": Ibid.

"They are good for me I've no doubt": Louisa May Alcott to Alfred Whitman, June 22, 1862, LMA, *Letters*, 79.

"I used to think that if Mr. Alcott's": Shealy, *Alcott in Her Own Time*, 8.

"Ah, he is too blue": Ibid., 11.

"sewing violently": Louisa May Alcott to Alfred Whitman, May 19, 1861, LMA, *Letters*, 64.

"She sent for me to make": LMA, *The Journals*, 105.

"The great parcel": Ibid.

"Spent our May-day": Ibid.

"Wrote, read, sewed": Ibid., 106.

"stick to your teaching": Ibid., 109.

"brainy, selfish, unladylike": Judith E. Harper, *Women During the Civil War: An Encyclopedia* (New York: Routledge, 2004), 275–277.

"Being willful, I said, 'I won't'": LMA, *The Journals*, 109.

"I will write 'great guns'": Louisa May Alcott to Alfred Whitman, November 12, 1861, LMA, *Letters*, 72.

"Last week was a busy, anxious time": Louisa May Alcott to the Alcott family, October 1858, LMA, *Letters*, 34.

"Miss Peabody has opened a 'Kinder Garten'": Louisa May Alcott to Alfred Whitman, November 12, 1862, LMA, *Letters*, 70.

"Very tired of this wandering life": LMA, *The Journals*, 108.

"I gave it up, as I could do": Ibid., 109.

"Though my tales are silly": Ibid.

"They are easier to 'compoze'": Louisa May Alcott to Alfred Whitman, June 22, 1862, LMA, *Letters*, 79.

"A dozen [stories] a month were easily turned": James Parton, *Noted Women of Europe and America: Authors, Artists, Reformers, and Heroines. Queens, Princesses, and Women of Society. Women Eccentric and Peculiar* (Hartford, CT: Phoenix, 1883), 84.

"Louisa and her sister Annie": Shealy, *Alcott in Her Own Time*, 82–83.

"a great taste for acting": Ibid., 91.

"Sewing Bees and Lint Picks 'our boys'": LMA, *The Journals*, 109.

"Our women appear to have become almost wild": "Correspondence. Duties of the Army Surgeon.—Females Not Suitable for Nurses," *American Medical Times* 3 (1861): 30.

"a monument of weak enthusiasts": Michael A. Flannery, *Civil War Pharmacy: A History of Drugs, Drug Supply and Provision, and Therapeutics for the Union and Confederacy* (New York: Pharmaceutical Products Press, 2004), 18.

"Miss Dix has been entrusted": William Grace, *The Army Surgeon's Manual: For the Use of Medical Officers, Cadets, Chaplains, and Hospital Stewards* (New York: Bailliere Brothers, 1864), 101.

"in her ministerings to the afflicted": "The United States General Hospital, Georgetown, D.C.," *Frank Leslie's Illustrated Newspaper*, July 6, 1861, 119.

"habits of neatness, order, sobriety": Rosamond Lamb, "A Great Woman of America: Dorothea Lynde Dix" (paper presented at the annual meeting of the Bostonian Society, Boston, Massachusetts, January 19, 1937).

"I want new experiences": LMA, *The Journals*, 110.

Chapter 3: A Soldier's Story

"a lady of culture": *Portrait and Biographical Record of Ford County, Illinois, Containing Biographical Sketches of Prominent and Representative Citizens, Together with Biographies of All the Governors of the State and of the Presidents of the United States* (Chicago: Lake City, 1892), 391.

"I told him if he needed any more": John F. Suhre, "My Dear Sister," October 6, 1862, Shure [sic] Letters, US Army Heritage and Education Center,

Carlisle, PA. Also published in its entirety in John Matteson, "Finding Private Suhre: On the Trail of Louisa May Alcott's 'Prince of Patients,'" *New England Quarterly* 83 (2015): 115. doi: 10.1162/TNEQ_a_00437.

"The dead are strewn so thickly": Frank Moore, ed., *The Civil War in Song and Story: 1860–1865* (New York: Peter Fenelon Collier, 1865), 473.

"In my feeble estimation": "Clara Barton at Antietam," National Park Service, last modified February 28, 2017, https://www.nps.gov/anti/learn/history culture/clarabarton.htm.

"I have, as you are aware, thought a great deal": Salmon P. Chase, *Diary and Correspondence of Salmon P. Chase* (Washington, DC: Government Printing Office, 1903), 87–88.

"I return thanks to our soldiers": "The President at Frederick, Maryland," *Evening Star*, October 6, 1862, 1, http://chroniclingamerica.loc.gov/lccn/sn83045462/1862-10-06/ed-1/seq-1/.

"As yet, no one except his constitutional advisors": *Alexandria Gazette*, October 6, 1862, 1. http://chroniclingamerica.loc.gov/lccn/sn85025007/1862-10-06/ed-1/seq-1.

"it would add to my comfort": Matteson, "Finding Private Suhre," 114–115.

"Give my love [to] Mother": Ibid., 115.

Chapter 4: Help Wanted

"I am getting ready to go to Washington": Louisa May Alcott to Mrs. Joseph Chatfield Alcox, LMA, *Letters*, 80.

"I reviewed every rag I possessed": L. M. Alcott, *Hospital Sketches* (Boston: James Redpath, 1863), 11.

"powerfully impatient": Ibid.

"Father writing & talking": Louisa May Alcott to Mrs. Joseph Chatfield Alcox, LMA, *Letters*, 80.

"Do you like ladies": Julian Hawthorne, "The Woman Who Wrote *Little Women*," *Ladies Home Journal*, October 1922, 120. Also in Julian Hawthorne, *The Memoirs of Julian Hawthorne*, ed. Edith Garrigues Hawthorne (New York: Macmillan, 1938), 68–71.

"My conceptions of bathing": Ibid.

"We and the Emersons often go": Ibid.

SOURCE NOTES

"The Alcott girls were society": Hawthorne, "The Woman Who Wrote *Little Women*," 120.

"Old Boys": Louisa May Alcott to Edward J. Bartlett and Garth Wilkinson James, December 4, 1862, LMA, *Letters*, 81.

"Wilkie was incomparable": Hawthorne, *Memoirs*, 121.

"I had been brought up in the belief": Garth W. James, "War Papers: The Assault on Fort Wagner" (paper presented at the Commandery of the State of Wisconsin, Military Order of the Loyal Legion of the United States, Milwaukee, Wisconsin, November 12, 1880).

"jollification & comfort": LMA, *Letters*, 81.

"Ned! Your sisters say": Ibid., 81.

"Now boys...If you intend to be smashed": Ibid., 82.

"The work is immensely hard": Massachusetts Historical Society. "Letter from Hannah Stevenson to Family and Friends, 8 August 1861." Accessed August 1, 2017. https://www.masshist.org/database/viewer.php?item_id=2163&pid=25.

"I cannot get over my surprise": Ibid.

"to be very careful, for you talk & laugh": Sarah Low Papers, 1844–1965, 1965.010, diary, pp. 13–14, New Hampshire Historical Society, Concord, NH.

"Miss Dix has nothing to do": Ibid., 17.

"Miss Dix has always been very insolent": Ibid., 12–13.

"They think so highly of Miss Stevenson": Ibid., 20.

"My old ankle will give out": Letter from Hannah Stevenson to Dearies [family], August 10, 1862, Ms. N-288, Box 5, Folders 12, 13, & 14, Curtis-Stevenson Family Papers, Hannah Elizabeth Stevenson Civil War Correspondence, 1862, Massachusetts Historical Society.

"a hard place": Louisa May Alcott, December 1862, LMA, *The Journals*, 110.

"Decided to go to Washington as nurse": Ibid.

"The Civil War so kindled her": Hawthorne, "The Woman Who Wrote *Little Women*," 120.

"You may begin at Plato": Matteson, *Eden's Outcasts*, 270.

"We catch glimpses of a dark mysterious": Louisa May Alcott to Adeline May, LMA, *Letters*, 57.

"I packed my 'go-abroady' possessions": Alcott, *Hospital Sketches*, 3.

"to the very mouth": Caroline Ticknor, *May Alcott: A Memoir* (Boston: Little, Brown, 1928), 54.

"I realized that I had": LMA, *The Journals*, 110.

Chapter 5: Georgetown or Bust

"I'm a bashful individual": Alcott, *Hospital Sketches*, 14.

"It was evident that I had made as absurd": Ibid.

"I turned desperate": Ibid.

"animated wet blanket": Ibid., 15.

"I'm going to Washington at five": Ibid., 16.

"I'm a woman's rights woman": Ibid., 17.

"I don't imagine he knew the anguish": Ibid., 19.

"A fat, easy gentleman": Ibid., 20.

"Appearances are proverbially deceitful": Daisy Eyebright, *A Manual of Etiquette with Hints on Politeness and Good Breeding* (Philadelphia: David McKay, 1868), 39.

"Having heard complaints of the absurd": Alcott, *Hospital Sketches*, 22.

"I put my bashfulness in my pocket": Ibid.

"We must secure our berths": Ibid., 23.

"If it ever intends to blow up": Ibid., 23–24.

"I've no intention of folding my hands": Ibid., 24.

"Think that my sandwiches": Ibid., 25.

"should enjoy throwing a stone": Ibid., 27.

"A most interesting journey into a new world": Louisa May Alcott, December 1862, LMA, *The Journals*, 110.

"I quite warmed to the excellent man": Alcott, *Hospital Sketches*, 27.

"We often passed colored people": Ibid., 28.

"Pennsylvania Avenue, with its bustle": Ibid., 30.

"I'll pay it out of my own pocket first": Margaret Leech, *Reveille in Washington, 1860–1865* (Garden City, NY: Garden City, 1945), 294.

"My poor boy. . . . He was too good": Brady Dennis, "Willie Lincoln's Death: A Private Agony for a President Facing a Nation of Pain," *Washington Post*,

October 7, 2011, accessed August 15, 2017, https://www.washingtonpost
.com/lifestyle/style/willie-lincolns-death-a-private-agony-for-a-president
-facing-a-nation-of-pain/2011/09/29/gIQAv7Z7SL_story.html?utm_term
=.ff0d5717daef.

"*A solemn time, but I'm glad*": LMA, *The Journals*, 110.

Chapter 6: Burnside's Blunder

"*By direction of the President of the United States, it is ordered*": The War of the Rebellion: A Compilation of the Official Records of the Union and Confederate Armies, series 1, vol. 21 (Washington, DC: Government Printing Office, 1888), 82.

"*The responsibility is so great*": Wilmer L. Jones, *Generals in Blue and Gray*, vol. 1: *Lincoln's Generals* (Mechanicsburg, PA: Stackpole Books, 2004), 152.

"*the most distressed man in the army*": Ibid.

"*Poor Burn feels dreadfully, almost crazy*": George B. McClellan to Mary Ellen McClellan, George B. McClellan, *The Civil War Papers of George B. McClellan*, ed. Stephen W. Sears (New York: Ticknor & Fields, 1989), 520.

"*The President has just assented to your plan*": War of the Rebellion, 84.

"*A chicken could not live on the field*": James Longstreet, "The Battle of Fredericksburg," in *Battles and Leaders of the Civil War*, Grant-Lee Edition, vol. 3, part 1 (New York: Century, 1888), 79.

"*The bombardment was terrific*": Warren Lee Goss, *Recollections of a Private: A Story of the Army of the Potomac* (New York: Thomas Y. Crowell, 1890), 123.

"*[In] the old mansion of Douglas Gordon*": *Alexandria Gazette*, December 17, 1862, 2.

"*The carrying out of your plan*": Jones, *Generals in Blue and Gray*, 160.

"*The action was close-handed and men fell*": National Park Service, "Battle of Fredericksburg History: Prospect Hill," accessed September 9, 2017, https://www.nps.gov/frsp/learn/historyculture/hist-fburg-prospect.htm.

"*like a steady dripping of rain*": Jones, *Generals in Blue and Gray*, 161.

"*Ye Gods! It is no longer a battle*": Ibid.

"Halt—lie down—you will all be killed": The Woman's Club of Mercersburg Pennsylvania, *Old Mercersburg* (New York: Frank Allaben Genealogical, 1912), 179.

"The stone wall was a sheet of flame": Andrew A. Humphreys, "Report of Brig. Gen. Andrew A. Humphreys, U.S. Army, Commanding Third Division," in *War of the Rebellion*, 432.

"a most terrific fire": Samuel P. Bates, *History of Pennsylvania Volunteers, 1861–1865*, vol. 4 (Harrisburg, PA: B. Singerly, State Printer, 1870), 264.

"the cries of the wounded rose up": Carol Reardon, "Humphrey's Pennsylvania Division," in *The Fredericksburg Campaign: Decision on the Rappahannock*, ed. Gary W. Gallagher (Chapel Hill: University of North Carolina Press, 1995), 99.

Chapter 7: The Hurly-Burly House

"I resigned myself to my fate": Alcott, *Hospital Sketches*, 70.

"care a fig": Hannah Stevenson to Dearies [family], September 17, 1862, Ms. N-288, Box 5, Folders 12, 13, & 14, Curtis-Stevenson Family Papers, Hannah Elizabeth Stevenson Civil War Correspondence.

"She is quite a feeble person": Hannah Stevenson to [family], July 21, 1862, Ms. N-288, Box 5, Folders 12, 13, & 14, Curtis-Stevenson Family Papers, Hannah Elizabeth Stevenson Civil War Correspondence.

"Why did you give this homely hen": Hannah Ropes, *Civil War Nurse: The Diary and Letters of Hannah Ropes*, ed. John R. Brumgardt (Knoxville: University of Tennessee Press, 1980), 12.

"loaded pistols and a bowie-knife": Ibid., 17.

"I take the place of his mother": Ibid., 15.

"jackal": Hannah Stevenson to Dearies [family], September 29, 1862, Ms. N-288, Box 5, Folders 12, 13, & 14, Curtis-Stevenson Family Papers, Hannah Elizabeth Stevenson Civil War Correspondence.

"walked around the ward": Ibid.

"Between surgeons, stewards, nurses and waiters": Ropes, *Civil War Nurse*, 69.

"gross inattention, rudeness to philanthropic": "The Alleged Abuses of Sick and Wounded Soldiers," *New York Daily Tribune*, September 19, 1862, 4.

"Food of the most miserable quality": Ibid.

"Surg[eon] Gen[eral] Hammond is said": Hannah Stevenson to Dearies [family], June 14, 1862, Ms. N-288, Box 5, Folders 12, 13, & 14, Curtis-Stevenson Family Papers, Hannah Elizabeth Stevenson Civil War Correspondence.

"As though I had not better business": Ropes, *Civil War Nurse*, 69.

"How I came to judge him": Ibid., 76–77.

"Call the Provost Marshall": Ibid., 81–85.

"If the thing should happen again": Ibid., 89.

"I wrote you all about her": Ibid., 59.

"Now, it would not do for you": Ibid., 61–62.

"The healing process is very slow": Ibid., 58.

"I sat looking at the twenty strong faces": December 1862, LMA, *The Journals*, 110.

"We get lousy!": Ropes, *Civil War Nurse*, 115–116.

"pneumonia on one side": Alcott, *Hospital Sketches*, 32.

"A strange day, but I did my best": December 1862, LMA, *The Journals*, 111.

"We are cheered by the arrival of Miss Alcott": Ropes, *Civil War Nurse*, 112.

"They've come, they've come! . . . It's the wounded from Fredericksburg": Alcott, *Hospital Sketches*, 31.

"I am free to confess": Ibid., 32.

"My ardor experienced a sudden chill": Ibid., 32–33.

"The hall was full of these wrecks": Ibid.

"The wounded are brought in": Robert Whitehouse, "Sarah Low Civil War Nurse," Dover Public Library, accessed October 18, 2017, http://www.dover.nh.gov/government/city-operations/library/history/sarah-low-civil-war-nurse.html.

"The sight of several stretchers": Alcott, *Hospital Sketches*, 34.

"with their clothes all on": Sarah Low to Aunt, September 1862, 1965.010, Sarah Low Papers, 1844–1965.

"I pitied them so much": Alcott, *Hospital Sketches*, 35.

"bigger than a pound of soap": Sarah Low Papers, 1844–1965, 1965.010, diary, p. 22.

"Wash as fast as you can": Alcott, *Hospital Sketches*, 35.

"If she had requested me to shave": Ibid.

"If I had come expecting to enjoy myself": "Letter from Louisa May Alcott to Hannah Stevenson, 26 December 1862," Massachusetts Historical Society, accessed August 1, 2017, http://www.masshist.org/database/2168.

"He was so overpowered by the honor": Alcott, *Hospital Sketches*, 35.

"I took heart and scrubbed away": Ibid., 36.

"The little Sergeant was merry": Ibid., 37.

"Now don't you fret yourself": Ibid.

"Being a red-hot Abolitionist": Ibid., 38.

"Shall I try to make you...No": Ibid.

"Thank you, ma'am...I don't think I'll ever eat": Ibid., 41.

"I laid a sheet over the quiet sleeper": Ibid., 42.

"He...seemed to regard a dilapidated body": Ibid., 42.

"He had a way of twitching off a bandage": Ibid., 97–98.

"The poor souls had to bear their pains": Ibid., 43.

"Be so good as to hold this...a strong desire to insinuate": Ibid., 98.

"was so mortified that the flesh dropped off": Whitehouse, "Sarah Low Civil War Nurse."

"It seems...the maggot actually does damage": C. Keith Wilbur, *Civil War Medicine 1861–1865* (Guilford, CT: Globe Pequot Press, 1998), 72.

"This I like to do for they put in such odd things": January 1863, LMA, *The Journals*, 114.

"I presently discovered that it took a very bad wound": Alcott, *Hospital Sketches*, 44.

"I find Mrs. Ropes very motherly": "Letter from Louisa May Alcott to Hannah Stevenson, 26 December 1862."

"By eleven, the last labor of love was done": Alcott, *Hospital Sketches*, 44.

"purely sympathetic": Ropes, *Civil War Nurse*, 121.

"Though often homesick, heartsick, and worn out": January 1863, LMA, *The Journals*, 114.

"The air is bad enough to breed a pestilence": LMA, *The Journals*, 114.

"continue to open doors and windows as if my life": Ibid.

"It is as much work to take care of 25 here": Sarah Low to her mother, September 25, 1862, 1965.010, Sarah Low Papers, 1844–1965.

"inevitable fried beef, salt butter, husky bread": LMA, *The Journals*, 114.

"the most faithful of workers": "Letter from Louisa May Alcott to Hannah Stevenson, 26 December 1862."

"a few very disagreeable women": LMA, *The Journals*, 114.

"the sanctified nurse who sung hymns & prayed violently": Louisa May Alcott to James Redpath, LMA, *Letters*, 93.

"Everything here strikes me as very odd": "Letter from Louisa May Alcott to Hannah Stevenson, 26 December 1862."

"both ludicrous and provoking": LMA, *The Journals*, 114.

"The conversation is entirely among themselves": Ibid.

"Gracious!...how can you?": Alcott, *Hospital Sketches*, 82.

"a dangerous fanatic": Ibid.

"The men would swear": Ibid., 81.

"murder ground": Ropes, *Civil War Nurse*, 114.

"soul-sickening slaughter": "The Disaster at Fredericksburg," *Bedford Gazette*, December 26, 1862, accessed July 7, 2017, http://chroniclingamerica.loc.gov/lccn/sn82005159/1862-12-26/ed-1/seq-2/.

"Burnside nobody blames": Ropes, *Civil War Nurse*, 114.

"The popular heart beats low": "Disaster at Fredericksburg."

"They wish to get rid of me": Orville Hickman Browning, December 1862, *The Diary of Orville Hickman Browning*, vol. 1, 1850–1864, ed. Theodore Calvin Pease and James G. Randall (Springfield: Trustees of the Illinois State Historical Library, 1925), 600.

"Although you were not successful": "President Lincoln's Address," *Alexandria Gazette*, December 24, 1862, accessed October 1, 2017, http://chroniclingamerica.loc.gov/lccn/sn85025007/1862-12-24/ed-1/seq-1/.

"full of amputated limbs": Ropes, *Civil War Nurse*, 116.

"Till noon I trot, trot": LMA, *The Journals*, 114.

"It is something like keeping house": Sarah Low to her mother, September 25, 1862.

"If we had capable attendants things would go nicely": "Letter from Louisa May Alcott to Hannah Stevenson, 26 December 1862."

"ghost from six in the morning": Ibid.

"I witnessed several operations": Alcott, *Hospital Sketches*, 96.

"*The amputation cases are dying*": Whitehouse, "Sarah Low Civil War Nurse."

"*Tables about breast high*": W. W. Blackford, *War Years with Jeb Stuart* (New York: Charles Scribner's Sons, 1945), 27–28.

"*The butchery practiced*": "News from Washington: Our Special Washington Dispatches," *New York Times*, December 25, 1862, 4.

"*I find him in a state of bliss*": Alcott, *Hospital Sketches*, 72.

"*My nerves belonged to the living*": Ibid., 97.

"*plain, odd, sentimental*": LMA, *The Journals*, 115.

"*Dr. John…goes purring about*": Ibid., 115.

"*Do I hurt you…all three laughed and talked*": Alcott, *Hospital Sketches*, 99.

"*Quotes Browning copiously*": LMA, *The Journals*, 115.

"*I like it, as it leaves me time for a morning run*": Ibid.

"*One, I visited armed with a dressing tray*": Alcott, *Hospital Sketches*, 47.

"*Many a jovial chat have I enjoyed*": Ibid., 93.

"*So just say that bit from Dickens*": Ibid.

"*Baby B., because he tended his arm*": Ibid., 94.

"*To tell the truth, I was a little afraid*": Ibid., 54–55.

"*I [have] never [been]…in a stranger place*": January 1863, LMA, *The Journals*, 113.

"*[The] topsey turvey letters [were] written*": Louisa May Alcott to Mary Elizabeth Waterman, LMA, *Letters*, 95.

"*jingled into [her] sleepy brain*": Louisa May Alcott to Annie Adams Fields, June 24, 1863, LMA, *Letters*, 84.

"*What is to be done? The good Doctor says*": Ropes, *Civil War Nurse*, 102.

"the family *of Georgetown*": Sarah Low Papers, 1844–1965, 1965.010, diary, p. 16.

"*Large quantities of provisions*": *Alexandria Gazette*, December 24, 1862, accessed November 18, 2017, http://chroniclingamerica.loc.gov/lccn/sn85025007/1862-12-24/ed-1/seq-1/.

"*We trimmed up the rooms*": "Letter from Louisa May Alcott to Hannah Stevenson, 26 December 1862."

"*Though what we call a common man*": LMA, *The Journals*, 113.

"*stony sort of room*": Ropes, *Civil War Nurse*, 118.

"fearful wound through the thigh": Ibid.

"Thoughtful and often beautifully mild": Alcott, *Hospital Sketches*, 55.

"Do you think I shall pull through": Ibid., 56.

"Every breath he draws...Bless you": Ibid.

"It was an easy thing for Dr. P.": Ibid., 56–57.

"I had seen many suffer": Ibid., 57.

"Let me help you bear it...I didn't like to be a trouble": Ibid.

"You shall not want": Ibid.

"Now I knew that to him": Ibid., 58.

"Our Christmas dinner was a funny scramble": "Letter from Louisa May Alcott to Hannah Stevenson, 26 December 1862."

"patients partook of a bounteous repast": "Christmas at the Hospitals," *Evening Star*, December 27, 1862.

"The turkeys and chickens were cut up": "The Hospital Christmas Dinners," *Evening Star*, December 26, 1862, accessed November 17, 2017, http://chroniclingamerica.loc.gov/lccn/sn83045462/1862-12-26/ed-1/seq-3/.

"While at the Armory Hospital": "Christmas in the Capital," *New York Herald*, December 26, 1862, accessed November 18, 1862, http://chroniclingamerica.loc.gov/lccn/sn83030313/1862-12-26/ed-1/seq-8/.

"The Christmas celebration was a great": Ropes, *Civil War Nurse*, 120.

"Your son is at the Union Hotel Hospital": The original letter is in the collection of the Historical & Genealogical Society of Somerset County, Inc., in Somerset, Pennsylvania, Accession ID number HS1966.1. The letter is also published in Matteson, "Finding Private Suhre," 105–106, 124.

"He is...mortally wounded & dying royally": January 1863, LMA, *The Journals*, 113.

"As if to assure himself that I was there": Alcott, *Hospital Sketches*, 59.

"Shall it be addressed to wife...Neither, ma'am": Ibid.

"We're not rich": Ibid.

"I wanted the right thing done": Ibid., 60.

"Do you ever regret...Never ma'am": Ibid.

"I'm not afraid": Ibid., 60–61.

"Shall I write to your mother...No, ma'am": Ibid., 61.

"John's was the best": LMA, *The Journals*, 114.

SOURCE NOTES

"I had been summoned to many death beds...I knew you'd come!": Alcott, *Hospital Sketches*, 62. In John Matteson's excellent article in the *New England Quarterly*, "Finding Private Suhre: On the Trail of Louisa May Alcott's 'Prince of Patients,'" he suggests that Louisa wasn't at John's beside when he died, based on his reading of Hannah Ropes's diary entry. I respectfully disagree with his interpretation.

"I saw the grey veil falling": Ibid.

"[The] ward physician is in his cups": Ropes, *Civil War Nurse*, 119.

"The man's soul seemed to sit": Alcott, *Hospital Sketches*, 62.

"There was in the man such a calm": Ropes, *Civil War Nurse*, 117–118.

"Thank you madam, I think I must be marching on": Ibid., 117.

"He never spoke again": Alcott, *Hospital Sketches*, 64.

"I could not but be glad that": Ibid.

"as though she would cross palms...wondrous manly beauty": Ropes, *Civil War Nurse*, 118.

"a tender sort of pride": Alcott, *Hospital Sketches*, 64.

"kissed this good son...glad to have known so genuine": Ibid., 65.

Chapter 8: A Bitter Pill

"My dear girl, we shall have you sick": Alcott, *Hospital Sketches*, 66.

"a frail young blossom": Ibid.

"Taking these things into consideration": Ibid., 67.

"The tax upon us women who work": Ropes, *Civil War Nurse*, 121.

"My last patient, who was so crazy": Ibid., 122.

"I have had the devoted attention": Ibid.

"No one had time to come up two flights": Alcott, *Hospital Sketches*, 68.

"Every morning I took a brisk run": Ibid., 71.

"long, clean, warm, and airy wards...cold, dirty, inconvenient": Ibid.

"memento of the respect and esteem": *Daily National Republican*, December 30, 1862, accessed July 25, 2018, http://chroniclingamerica.loc.gov/lccn/sn86053570/1862-12-30/ed-1/seq-3/.

"Here [at the Armory Square Hospital], order, method, common sense": Ibid., 71–72.

SOURCE NOTES

"the furniture, though extremely rich": "Downstairs at the White House: Blue Room," Lehrman Institute, accessed December 7, 2017, http://www .mrlincolnswhitehouse.org/the-white-house/downstairs-at-the-white-house/ downstairs-white-house-blue-room.

"sunken, deathly look": Noah Brooks, *Mr. Lincoln's Washington: Selections from the Writings of Noah Brooks, Civil War Correspondent*, ed. P. J. Staudenraus (South Brunswick, NJ: Thomas Yoseloff, 1967), 29.

"Mrs. Lincoln told me": Browning, *Diary*, 608.

"He lives...He comes to me every night": Terry Alford, "The Spiritualist Who Warned Lincoln Was Also Booth's Drinking Buddy," *Smithsonian Magazine*, March 2015, accessed December 14, 2017, https://www .smithsonianmag.com/history/the-spiritualist-who-warned-lincoln-was -also-booths-drinking-buddy-180954317.

"it had been dragged": Noah Brooks, *Washington in Lincoln's Time* (New York: Century, 1895), 67.

"I never, in my life, felt more certain": Frederick W. Seward, *Seward at Washington as Senator and Secretary of State: A Memoir of His Life, with Selections from His Letters, 1861–1872* (New York: Derby and Miller, 1891), 151.

"I have been sick, or you should have": Ropes, *Civil War Nurse*, 121.

"keep merry": December 1862, LMA, *The Journals*, 115.

"stuffed fowls...perambulating flower bed": Alcott, *Hospital Sketches*, 78.

"I was learning...what the men suffer and sigh": Ibid., 77.

"My sister nurses fed me": Ibid., 76.

"Miss Dix does not allow": Ropes, *Civil War Nurse*, 123.

"one long fight with weariness": Alcott, *Hospital Sketches*, 83.

"I ought to have risen up and thanked him": Ibid., 100.

"I feel no better": January 1863, LMA, *The Journals*, 115.

"The idea of giving up so soon": Alcott, *Hospital Sketches*, 84.

"like a welcome ghost": Ibid.

"Was amazed to see Father": LMA, *The Journals*, 116.

"Letters come from Louisa": Alcott, January 1863, *The Journals of Bronson Alcott*, 352.

"*out of the dangers*": Bronson Alcott, *The Letters of A. Bronson Alcott*, ed.
Richard L. Herrnstadt (Ames: Iowa State University Press, 1969), 333.

"*kind soul...No one likes her*": LMA, *The Journals*, 116, 123.

"*Horrid war*": Bronson Alcott, *The Journals of Bronson Alcott*, 353.

"*I sit near the President*": Ibid.

"*Mrs. Ropes was a remarkable character*": Ropes, *Civil War Nurse*, 125.

"*Everyone about the place looked up*": Ibid., 126–127.

"*I have been unhappy at not having Mrs. Ropes*": Ibid., 126.

"*I love you very much but feel*": Ibid., 127–128.

"*Mother was near me last night*": Ibid., 128.

Chapter 9: Duty's Faithful Daughter

"*Father is there & she is recovering*": Abby May (Alcott) Nierecker, 1840–1879,
A.MS, diary [v.p.] September 1 1852–July 25 1863, p. 82, Louisa May Al-
cott additional papers, 1845–1944, MS Am 1817 (56), Houghton Library,
Harvard University, Cambridge, MA.

"*She is very cross*": Ibid., 83.

"*I was greatly shocked*": Ibid.

"*Louisa was faint*": Alcott, *The Letters of A. Bronson Alcott*, 333.

"*had a sort of fit...a dreadful time of it*": LMA, *The Journals*, 116.

"*Louisa was communicative*": Ibid.

"*Poor Louy...She left us a brave*": Abigail May Alcott to Samuel Joseph
May, 1863, MS Am 1130.0(28), Amos Bronson Alcott papers, 1799–1888,
Houghton Library, Harvard University, Cambridge, MA.

"*All of us are very anxious*": Nierecker, diary, 84.

"*Dr. Bartlett has seen her*": Alcott, *The Letters of A. Bronson Alcott*, 333.

"*I hate Drs. and all their nonsense*": Matteson, *Eden's Outcasts*, 287.

"*The efficacy of good nursing*": Ibid.

"*Neither she nor father like to have me*": Nierecker, diary, 84.

"*Louisa is here at home again*": Bronson Alcott, *The Letters of A. Bronson
Alcott*, 333.

"*Lie still, my dear*": January 1863, LMA, *The Journals*, 116.

"*She dreads the fever fits*": Alcott, *The Letters of A. Bronson Alcott*, 334.

"*The Dr. pronounced her*": Ibid.

"Mother giving out": Nierecker, diary, 84.

"insurmountable calamity...fierce campaign": Sophia Peabody Hawthorne to Annie Fields, "Hawthorne, Sophia, 1809–1871 autograph letter signed to Annie Adams Fields, [Concord, 20] February 1863," manuscript, February 20, 1863, *Digital Commonwealth*, accessed January 12, 2018, http://ark.digitalcommonwealth.org/ark:/50959/wh247j09p.

"She asked me to sit near her": Alcott, *The Letters of A. Bronson Alcott*, 334.

"If you will only take that man away": Sophia Peabody Hawthorne to Annie Fields, February 20, 1863, *Digital Commonwealth*. http://ark.digital commonwealth.org/ark:/50959/wh247j09p.

"How could you leave me": Ibid.

"Was told I had had a very bad": LMA, *The Journals*, 117.

"Never having been sick": Ibid.

"Had all my hair, 1 1/2 yard long": Ibid.

"We trust the main perils are past": Alcott, *The Letters of A. Bronson Alcott*, 335.

"Active exercise was my delight": Alcott, *Louisa May Alcott: Her Life, Letters, and Journals*, 30.

"Such long, long nights": LMA, *The Journals*, 117.

"Tried to sew; read & write": Ibid.

"had not detected the secrets": Sophia Peabody Hawthorne to Annie Fields. February 20, 1863.

"decidedly better": Ibid.

"Louy down stairs & dressed": Nierecker, diary, 84.

"rack a bones": Louisa May Alcott to Anna Alcott Pratt, March 30, 1863, LMA, *Letters*, 83.

"Falling back in my old ways": LMA, *The Journals*, 117.

"Good news!...Anna has": Louisa May Alcott to Mary Elizabeth Waterman, November 6, 1863, LMA, *Letters*, 94.

"With one accord, we three opened": Ibid.

"Father brought the good news": Nierecker, diary, 86.

"I fell to cleaning house": LMA, *The Journals*, 118.

"Sanborn asked me to do": Ibid.

"Felt as if born again": Ibid.

SOURCE NOTES

"*I never shall regret the going*": Alcott, *Hospital Sketches*, 84.

"*That was our contribution*": Alcott, *The Letters of A. Bronson Alcott*, 336.

Chapter 10: A Gift

"*People mustn't talk about genius*": Louisa May Alcott to James Redpath, February 1864, LMA, *Letters*, 79.

"*Let me tell you what extreme pleasure*": Ibid., 94.

"*I am so delighted with your*": Madeleine B. Stern, *Critical Essays on Louisa May Alcott* (Boston: G. K. Hall, 1984), 28.

"*Much to my surprise*": April 1863, LMA, *The Journals*, 118.

"*I find I've done a good thing*": LMA, *The Journals*, 122.

"*The contrast between comic incidents*": Stern, *Critical Essays on Louisa May Alcott*, 25.

"*'A Night' was much liked*": LMA, *The Journals*, 118.

"*inverted tin kettles*": Louisa May Alcott to Mary Elizabeth Waterman, November 6, 1863, LMA, *Letters*, 95.

"*One gets acquainted with her*": Nierecker, diary, 83.

"*I preferred Redpath & said yes*": LMA, *The Journals*, 119.

"*I too am sure the 'he who giveth'*": LMA, *Letters*, 86–87.

"*Upon quietly reading it to myself*": Sophia Peabody Hawthorne to Annie Fields, June 14, 1863, *Digital Commonwealth*, http://ark.digitalcommonwealth.org/ark:/50959/wh247j79c.

"*Of course I didn't say No*": LMA, *The Journals*, 119.

"*I have every blessing*": Nierecker, diary, 93.

"*I am growing very old*": Ibid., 96.

"*pleasant people…boating, singing, dancing*": LMA, *The Journals*, 119.

"*How generous Louisa is*": Nierecker, diary, 96.

"*I cannot work very steadily*": LMA, *Letters*, 89.

"*My first morning glory bloomed*": LMA, *The Journals*, 120.

"*I see nothing in the way*": Alcott, January 1863, *The Journals of Bronson Alcott*, 357.

"*The wealth of curious humor*": "New Books: Hospital Sketches," *Daily Green Mountain Freeman*, November 9, 1863, accessed November 24, 2017, http://chroniclingamerica.loc.gov/lccn/sn84023210/1863-11-09/ed-1/seq-2/.

"*I have the satisfaction of seeing*": LMA, *Letters*, 88.

"*as jolly as ever*": LMA, *Letters*, 92, 95.

"*To say that I thank you for writing*": Stern, *Critical Essays on Louisa May Alcott*, 28. (The surgeon was not identified by name.)

"*I should like of all things*": LMA, *Letters*, 96.

"*Mr. Philbrick objected*": Ibid. Philbrick is spelled Philbrey in her letter.

"*I proudly paid out of my story money*": LMA, *The Journals*, 125.

"*If ever there was an astonished*": Ibid., 121.

"*He now lies on a sofa*": LMA, *The Journals*, 121.

"*Your wonderful little book*": LMA, *Letters*, 94.

"*Was 31 on the 29th*": LMA, *The Journals*, 121.

"*Short-sighted, Louisa!*": Alcott, *Louisa May Alcott: Her Life, Letters, and Journals*, 152.

Chapter 11: Unfulfilled Destiny

"*Hearing that I was something of a nurse*": Louisa May Alcott, July 1865, LMA, *The Journals*, 141.

"*I missed my freedom*": Ibid., 144.

"*We walked a little, talked a little, bathed*": Ibid., 142.

"*I tried my best to suit & serve her*": Ibid.

"*The book was hastily got out*": Ibid., 133.

"*Being tired of novels, I soon dropped it*": Ibid., 139.

"*All is happy & well, thank God!*": Ibid., 142.

"*Thoroughly beaten, I could not wonder*": Louisa May Alcott, *The Sketches of Louisa May Alcott* (Forest Hills, NY: Ironweed Press, 2001), 177.

"*A church to Almighty God*": Ibid., 181.

"*That boy is sick and needs care*": Alcott, *Aunt Jo's Scrap-Bag*, 18.

"*I drink the good health*": Ibid., 17.

"*So simple, frank and grateful was he*": Ibid., 18.

"*With his fellow students he had fought*": Louisa May Alcott, *Little Women*, ed. Anne Hiebert Alton (Ontario: Broadview Press, 2001), 532.

"*and manfully began the hard fight*": Ibid.

"*Play me the forbidden hymn*": Ibid.

"*I look to see if the baron is here*": Ibid.

"*Then play it*": Ibid.

"*Ah, mademoiselle . . . It is true we are enemies*": Ibid.

"*for giving me a lesson*": Ibid.

"*From that evening we were fast friends*": Ibid.

"*her wrongs with the simple eloquence*": Alcott, *Sketches of Louisa May Alcott*, 179.

"*The tables were completely turned*": Ibid.

"*all good & happiness on earth*": LMA, *The Journals*, 145.

"*A little romance with L[adislas] W[eisneiwsky]*": Ibid.

"*I do not say adieu but au revoir*": Alcott, *Little Women*, 533.

"*Very tired of doing nothing pleasant*": LMA, *The Journals*, 145.

"*Anna was troubled about Laddie*": Ibid.

"*My time is too valuable to be spent fussing*": Ibid., 150.

"*as happy as a freed bird*": Ibid., 151.

"*You are better?*": Alcott, *Aunt Jo's Scrap-Bag*, 24.

"*I truly hope so . . . The winter was good*": Ibid.

"*couldn't be*": LMA, *The Journals*, 148.

"*If in my present life if I love*": Louisa May Alcott, "Louisa May Alcott's Letters to Five Girls," *Ladies Home Journal* 13, no. 5 (April 1896).

Chapter 12: The Chariot of Glory

"*Mr. Niles wants a girls' story*": Louisa May Alcott, May 1868, LMA, *The Journals*, 165.

"*The money-maker was away*": Alcott, *Louisa May Alcott: Her Life, Letters, and Journals*, 184.

"*Got to work . . . for bills accumulate*": Ibid., 185–186.

"*Alas! I wish, for her*": Alcott, January 1863, *The Journals of Bronson Alcott*, 362.

"*I never expect to see the strong*": Alcott, *Louisa May Alcott: Her Life, Letters, and Journals*, 185.

"*I begin 'Little Women'*": Ibid., 198–199.

"*He thought it dull . . . lively, simple books*": Ibid., 199.

"*Very tired, head full of pain*": Ibid.

"It reads better than I expected": Ibid.

"Saw Mr. Niles": Ibid., 200–201.

"Girls write to ask who the little women marry": Ibid., 201.

"'Jo' should have remained": Louisa May Alcott to Elizabeth Powell, March 10, [1869], LMA, *Letters*, 124–125.

"I am so full of my work": Alcott, *Louisa May Alcott: Her Life, Letters, and Journals*, 201.

"I never seem to have many presents,": LMA, *The Journals*, 167.

"Paid up all the debts": Alcott, *Louisa May Alcott: Her Life, Letters, and Journals*, 202.

"quite used up. Don't care for myself": Ibid.

"With that thought I can bear": LMA, *The Journals*, 172.

"left hand in a sling, one foot up": Alcott, *Louisa May Alcott: Her Life, Letters, and Journals*, 209.

"Many thanks for the check": LMA, *Letters*, 129.

"I am introduced as the father of Little Women": Alcott, *The Journals of Bronson Alcott*, 404.

"Gifted Sire of Louisa M. Alcott!": LMA, *The Journals*, 198.

"As a poor, proud, struggling girl": Alcott, "Louisa May Alcott's Letters to Five Girls."

Epilogue: Back on the Front Lines

"He has his dream realized at last": Louisa May Alcott, July 1879, LMA, *The Journals*, 215.

"If [women] can emancipate the slave": Abigail May Alcott, *My Heart Is Boundless*, 212.

"a great warmth seems gone out of life": LMA, *The Journals*, 206.

"wonderfully indifferent": Alcott, *My Heart Is Boundless*, 212.

"I like to help women help themselves": Alcott, "Louisa May Alcott's Letters to Five Girls."

"Very informal meetings, where we met and talked": Louisa May Alcott to the *Woman's Journal*, October 11, 1879, LMA, *Letters*, 238.

"I am ashamed to say": Ibid.

SOURCE NOTES

"*So hard to move people*": LMA, *The Journals*, 216.

"*I have words in favor of Woman Suffrage*": Alcott, August 11, 1879, *The Journals of Bronson Alcott*, 508.

"*No bolt fell on our audacious heads*": LMA, *The Letters*, 246.

"*looked disturbed*": Ibid.

"*We elected a good school committee*": LMA, *The Journals*, 225.

"*The ice is broken*": LMA, *The Letters*, 247.

"*If I can do no more, let my name stand*": Louisa May Alcott, "Miss Alcott on Woman Suffrage," *New York Times*, October 28, 1885, 2.

SELECTED BIBLIOGRAPHY

Alcott, Abigail May. *My Heart Is Boundless: Writings of Abigail May Alcott, Louisa's Mother.* Edited by Eve LaPlante. New York: Free Press, 2012.

Alcott, Amos Bronson. Amos Bronson Alcott Papers. Houghton Library, Harvard University, Cambridge, MA.

——. *The Journals of Amos Bronson Alcott.* Edited by Odell Shepard. Boston: Little, Brown, 1938.

——. *The Letters of A. Bronson Alcott.* Edited by Richard L. Herrnstadt. Ames: Iowa State University Press, 1969.

Alcott, Louisa May. *Flower Fables.* Boston: George W. Briggs, 1854. Accessed January 23, 2018. https://archive.org/details/flowerfables00alcoiala.

——. *Hospital Sketches.* Boston: James Redpath, 1863. Accessed January 23, 2018. https://archive.org/details/hospitalsketches00alcorich.

——. *The Journals of Louisa May Alcott.* Edited by Joel Myerson and Daniel Shealy. Introduction by Madeleine B. Stern. Athens: University of Georgia Press, 1997.

——. *Little Women.* Edited by Anne Hiebert Alton. Ontario: Broadview Press, 2001.

——. *Little Women, or Meg, Jo, Beth and Amy.* Illustrations by May Alcott. Boston: Roberts Brothers, 1869. Accessed January 28, 2018. https://archive.org/details/littlewomenormeg01alco.

——. *Little Women, or Meg, Jo, Beth and Amy. Part Second.* Boston: Roberts Brothers, 1869. Accessed January 28, 2018. https://archive.org/details/littlewomen00alco_9.

——. *Louisa May Alcott, Her Life, Letters, and Journals.* Edited by Ednah D. Cheney. Carlisle, MA: Applewood Books, 1889.

——. Louisa May Alcott Papers. Houghton Library, Harvard University, Cambridge, MA.

——. *Moods: A Novel.* Boston: Roberts Brothers, 1881. Accessed January 23, 2018. https://archive.org/details/moodsnovel1882alco.

——. *The Selected Letters of Louisa May Alcott.* Edited by Joel Myerson and Daniel Shealy. Introduction by Madeleine B. Stern. Athens: University of Georgia Press, 1995.

——. *The Sketches of Louisa May Alcott.* Introduction by Gregory Eiselein. New York: Ironweed Press, 2001.

——. *Work: A Story of Experience.* Boston: Roberts Brothers, 1873. [Working title was *Success.*] Accessed January 23, 2018. https://archive.org/details/workstoryofexper1873alco.

Anthony, Katharine. *Louisa May Alcott.* New York: Alfred A. Knopf, 1938.

Barton, Cynthia H. *Transcendental Wife: The Life of Abigail May Alcott.* Lanham, MD: University Press of America, 1996.

Brooks, Noah. *Mr. Lincoln's Washington: Selections from the Writings of Noah Brooks, Civil War Correspondent.* Edited by P. J. Staudenraus. South Brunswick, NJ: Thomas Yoseloff, 1967.

——. *Washington in Lincoln's Time.* New York: Century, 1896.

Dyer, J. Franklin. *The Journal of a Civil War Surgeon.* Edited by Michael B. Chesson. Lincoln: University of Nebraska Press, 2003.

Eiselein, Gregory, and Anne K. Phillips, eds. *The Louisa May Alcott Encyclopedia.* Foreword by Madeleine B. Stern. Westport, CT: Greenwood Press, 2001.

Ellis, John B. *The Sights and Secrets of the National Capital: A Work Descriptive of Washington City in All Its Various Phases.* New York: Trow & Smith, 1869.

Emerson, Ellen Tucker. *The Letters of Ellen Tucker Emerson.* Vol. 1. Edited by Edith E. W. Gregg. Foreword by Gay Wilson Allen. Kent, OH: Kent State University Press, 1982.

Gowing, Clara. *The Alcotts as I Knew Them.* Boston: C. M. Clarke, 1909.

Harper, Judith E. *Women During the Civil War: An Encyclopedia.* Foreword by Elizabeth D. Leonard. New York: Routledge, 2004.

Hawthorne, Julian. *The Memoirs of Julian Hawthorne*. Edited by Edith Garrigues Hawthorne. New York: Macmillan, 1938.

——. *Nathaniel Hawthorne and His Wife: A Biography*. Vol. 2. Boston: James R. Osgood, 1884.

Hawthorne, Sophia Peabody. Sophia Peabody Hawthorne Collection of Papers. New York Public Library Archives and Manuscripts.

Hirschhorn, Norbert, and Ian A. Greaves. "Louisa May Alcott: Her Mysterious Illness." *Perspectives in Biology and Medicine* 50, no. 2 (Spring 2007): 243–259.

Lothrop, Margaret M. *The Wayside: Home of Authors*. New York: American Book, 1968.

Low, Sarah. Sarah Low Papers. New Hampshire Historical Society, Concord, NH.

Matteson, John. *Eden's Outcasts: The Story of Louisa May Alcott and Her Father*. New York: W. W. Norton, 2007.

——. "Finding Private Suhre: On the Trail of Louisa May Alcott's 'Prince of Patients.'" *New England Quarterly* 83 (2015): 104–125. Accessed December 15, 2016. doi: 10.1162/TNEQ_a_00437.

Morrow, Honoré Willsie. *The Father of Little Women*. Boston: Little, Brown, 1927.

Nightingale, Florence. *Notes on Nursing: What It Is, and What It Is Not*. Foreword by Virginia M. Dunbar. Preface by Margaret B. Dolan. New York: Dover, 1969.

Reisen, Harriet. *Louisa May Alcott: The Woman Behind Little Women*. New York: Picador, 2009.

Ropes, Hannah Anderson. *Civil War Nurse: The Diary and Letters of Hannah Ropes*. Edited with an introduction and commentary by John R. Brumgardt. Knoxville: University of Tennessee Press, 1980.

Scudder, Townsend. *Concord: American Town*. Boston: Little, Brown, 1947.

Shealy, Daniel, ed. *Alcott in Her Own Time*. Iowa City: University of Iowa Press, 2005.

Shepard, Odell. *Pedlar's Progress: The Life of Bronson Alcott*. Boston: Little, Brown, 1937.

Stern, Madeleine B. *Critical Essays on Louisa May Alcott*. Boston: G. K. Hall, 1984.

———. *Louisa May Alcott: A Biography*. Boston: Northeastern University Press, 1996.

———. "Louisa M. Alcott: Civil War Nurse." *Americana* 37 (1943): 296–325.

Stevenson, Hannah. Curtis-Stevenson Family Papers. Massachusetts Historical Society, Boston, MA.

Ticknor, Caroline. *May Alcott: A Memoir*. Boston: Little, Brown, 1928.

Wilbur, C. Keith. *Civil War Medicine 1861–1865*. Guilford, CT: Globe Pequot Press, 1998.

Woodward, Joseph Janvier. *The Hospital Steward's Manual: For the Instruction of Hospital Stewards, Ward-Masters, and Attendants, in Their Several Duties*. Philadelphia: J. B. Lippincott, 1863.

INDEX

INDEX

Alcott, Anna (*cont.*)

  personality of, 15, 23, 51

  visit to recuperating Louisa, 151

Alcott, Beth "Lizzie," 23, 26–27,

  123, 151

Alcott, Bronson

  appreciation for Louisa's

    strengths, 147, 155

  belief in virtues of pears, 55–56

  daughter's success and, 190–191

  educational reform beliefs of, 13

  education of, 12–13

  as father, 14–15

  feminism and, 1

  Fruitlands and, 16–18

  fugitive slave and, 10

  hearing Lincoln speak, 138–139

  helping nurse ailing Louisa,

    146, 147

  inability to support family, 2,

    18–19, 32, 173, 186

  journey home with ailing Louisa,

    142, 144–145

  lecture tours, 21, 186, 190–191

  on Louisa's condition with

    typhoid, 146, 148

  on Louisa's recovery, 150

  meeting and marrying Abba,

    19–20

  narcissism of, 20

  publication of *Tablets*, 186, 189

  regret over Louisa's work in war,

    155

  relationship with Louisa, 14–15,

    23, 147, 155

  School of Philosophy, 193, 195

  as school superintendent, 31–32,

    33, 173

  as schoolteacher, 12, 13

  seeing Louisa off on train to

    Washington, 56–57

  showing "Thoreau's Flute" to

    Sophia Hawthorne, 161

  support for women's suffrage,

    195

  transcendentalism and, 11–12

  visit to Anna and baby, 153

  in Washington to bring ailing

    Louisa home, 137–139, 144

Alcott, Louisa May "Lu"

  abolitionism and, 1, 102–103, 166

  as actress, 36–37

  administering kindergarten, 35

  advancing cause of human rights,

    164–165

  attempts to win parents' approval,

    22

  birthdays, 53, 166, 180, 189

  Bronson's discipline of, 14

  calomel treatment and, 136, 150

  campaign for women's suffrage

    and, 193–197

  Christmases, 7–8, 113–115, 118–119,

    166–167, 181, 190

  as companion to Anna Weld,

    171–175, 180–181, 181–182

INDEX

INDEX

INDEX

INDEX